ENGAGING
STUDENTS WITH
poverty
IN MIND

ERIC JENSEN

ENGAGING
STUDENTS WITH
poverty
IN MIND

PRACTICAL STRATEGIES
FOR RAISING ACHIEVEMENT

 | Alexandria, Virginia

1703 N. Beauregard St. • Alexandria, VA 22311-1714 USA
Phone: 800-933-2723 or 703-578-9600 • Fax: 703-575-5400
Website: www.ascd.org • E-mail: member@ascd.org
Author guidelines: www.ascd.org/write

Gene R. Carter, *Executive Director;* Mary Catherine (MC) Desrosiers, *Chief Program Development Officer;* Richard Papale, *Publisher;* Laura Lawson, *Acquisitions Editor;* Julie Houtz, *Director, Book Editing & Production;* Miriam Goldstein, *Editor;* Sima Nasr, *Senior Graphic Designer;* Mike Kalyan, *Production Manager;* Keith Demmons, *Desktop Publishing Specialist;* Kyle Steichen, *Production Specialist*

Printed in the United States of America. Cover art © 2013 by ASCD. ASCD publications present a variety of viewpoints. The views expressed or implied in this book should not be interpreted as official positions of the Association.

All web links in this book are correct as of the publication date below but may have become inactive or otherwise modified since that time. If you notice a deactivated or changed link, please e-mail books@ascd.org with the words "Link Update" in the subject line. In your message, please specify the web link, the book title, and the page number on which the link appears.

PAPERBACK ISBN: 978-1-4166-1572-9   ASCD product #113001   n8/13
Also available as an e-book (see Books in Print for the ISBNs).

Quantity discounts: 10–49 copies, 10%; 50+ copies, 15%; for 1,000 or more copies, call 800-933-2723, ext. 5773, or 703-575-5773. For desk copies: www.ascd.org/deskcopy

Library of Congress Cataloging-in-Publication Data

Jensen, Eric, 1950-
  Engaging students with poverty in mind : practical strategies for raising achievement / Eric Jensen.
       pages cm
  Includes bibliographical references and index.
  ISBN 978-1-4166-1572-9 (pbk. : alk. paper) 1. Poor children--Education--United States. 2. Academic achievement--United States. 3. Motivation in education--United States. I. Title.
  LC4091.J46 2013
  371.826'94--dc23
                        2013017847

22 21 20 19 18   7 8 9 10 11 12

ENGAGING
STUDENTS WITH
poverty
IN MIND

Acknowledgments

I am very grateful for editorial and research support from Nanette Metz, Ruth Fine, and Pam Rooks. I am continually indebted to professional contributions from Jean Blaydes, Bryan Harris, LeAnn Nickelsen, and Rich Allen. I am also grateful for the editors and publisher at ASCD, who have been very supportive of this project, and Miriam Goldstein, who has made incalculable contributions with her thoughtful editing.

Finally, my wife, Diane, is always supportive of my writing projects and is a never-ending blessing.

Preface

Looking at this book's title, maybe you're wondering about a couple of things. What would I know about this subject? What gives me, a middle-class white guy, the right to do a book on poverty? A skeptical teacher actually e-mailed me these questions. I think they are valid, and I'll answer them with a short story about a real kid.

This boy's first memory was of standing in the living room of his house at age 2. Tears streamed down his cheeks. His mother sheepishly walked out the front door. It was the day the divorce went through. Four tumultuous years later, his father remarried for the second of four times. The first of the boy's three stepmothers was alcoholic and abusive. Both of his older sisters quickly moved out of the house, one to live with neighbors and the other to live in the garage.

At home, the young boy often ate dog food for snacks between meals because he was locked out of the house. From 2nd through 10th grade, he was terrorized by his violent stepmother. Blood and broken glass were commonplace in the house. Every time things got *really* bad, the father moved the boy and his sister to stay with relatives. Then the boy's stepmother would promise to be better, and the trio would move back. The boy lived with his grandmother, his aunt, his uncle, and then on his own. The cycle repeated itself every couple of years. School was a confusing and disconnected process. During those turbulent years, he went to nine schools and had 153 teachers.

The boy wasn't at any school long enough to develop real friendships. He was often truant and frequently got sent to the office for discipline issues. In class, he usually sat at the back, troubled and disconnected from the content. Mostly, he thought about what it was going to be like when he got home. For him, home was a war zone. Getting homework done was impossible in his environment. He had zero parental support, and his only friends were troublemakers. His dad was gone most of the time, going to night school and often spending weekends working in the National Guard. His dad was also engaged in an affair, which made for even more friction and accusations at home.

Why am I telling you about this child's upbringing? What do these experiences have to do with this book?

This is the true story of my own childhood. I'm not asking for sympathy. My upbringing was not of my choosing, so I accept neither credit nor blame. This is just a brief edited piece of my life story. (The reality was not nearly so G-rated.) My point is this: don't judge someone by his or her skin color, ethnicity, or socioeconomic status.

Just because I grew up white and middle-class does not mean I don't understand the "real world." I've been arrested twice and had eight near-death experiences. I lived in a laundry room for two years and in a 15-foot trailer for five years. I've been kidnapped and held at gunpoint. I've been robbed, I've been a stowaway, and I've had to ride boxcars for over 1,000 miles to get home. I understand what it's like for the kid sitting in the back of the room who can't focus and spends the class worrying about what might happen when he goes home. I know what it's like to be hungry all the time. I was one of those kids.

Teaching students who live in poverty—especially teaching in a school with a high-poverty student population, like a Title I school—exposes every single weakness a teacher has. If you don't learn, adapt, build relationships, and bring your A-game every single day, your class will be a living hell. If you're adaptive, if you dream big, if you care a lot, and if the impossible doesn't scare you, then your students will pick up on that and respect you. How do I know? Two middle school teachers made that difference in my life. They showed me empathy. They challenged me to do better, and they engaged me in class. I became a teacher because of them. I learned to focus, write, and learn—and then to learn again, from my mistakes. Teachers can make a real difference in the lives of students who face continual adversity.

Some teachers tell me, "Those kids just need more discipline. You have to show them who's in charge." It doesn't work that way. First, they are not "those kids"; they are *our* kids. The future of the United States depends on whether or not these kids succeed. They need loving, caring role models, not prison guards.

Second, if you want high-performing students, you must be willing to become a high-performing teacher. Stop pointing fingers and making excuses. Every student would rather have a caring, engaging teacher than a finger-pointer. The attitudes and strategies of yesterday are not enough anymore. It's time to upgrade your teaching.

Why am I encouraging you to set your own bar so high? If you're like most educators, it's likely you're pretty engaged with your work. You participate in meetings, take care of logistics, make phone calls and write e-mails, plan lessons, administer tests, and engage in a host of other activities. But what if you set the bar higher for your own classroom? I'm not saying, "Work more hours." I am saying, "What if your new bar was to reach far more students in far more engaging and profound ways?" How engaging is today for every single one of your students?

You won't ever get good at your job if you stay the same. You'll still have underperforming students, and they will see through you with X-ray eyes. Teaching is easy; teaching *well* is hard work. If the only change you want to make is to add a few cutesy strategies, this book is not for you.

The truth is, teaching students well will change you. Let me repeat that: *teaching well will change you.* This book will enable you to understand the students you work with in new ways that will help you to help them succeed. If you are ready to take that journey, fasten your seat belt. It's going to be a wild ride.

Introduction

The academic record of students who live in poverty is not good. In the United States, if you are poor, your odds of graduating are lower than are those of a middle-income student. If you are also Hispanic or black, your odds just dropped again. Half of all poor students of color drop out of school (Alliance for Excellent Education, 2008). Seventy percent of all children who do not graduate from high school have spent at least a year living in poverty (Hernandez, 2012). In 2009, the dropout rate of students living in low-income families was about five times greater than the rate of students from high-income families: 7.4 percent versus 1.4 percent (Chapman, Laird, Ifill, & KewalRamani, 2011).

This is not a failure within the students. There are no poor students with deficits; there are only broken schools that need fixing. There are no failing students; there are only schools that are failing our students. There are no unmotivated students; there are only teachers whose classrooms are frightfully boring, uncaring, or irrelevant. Such classrooms fail to engage students enough to be able to meet their needs. If you think these are outrageous statements, this book is for you. I'll show you the evidence and share the success stories.

Engagement Matters

Engagement shows up as a vital achievement factor in most studies, although it's not always explicitly called *engagement;* sometimes it's "disguised" as feedback, cooperative learning, project learning, or interactive teaching (Hattie, 2008). The correlation between student engagement and achievement is consistently strong and significant: research shows that for every 2 percent disengagement rises, pass rates on high-stakes tests drop by 1 percent (Valentine & Collins, 2011).

Students love being engaged, and they value engagement *very* highly (Appleton, Christenson, & Furlong, 2008). Engagement is especially important for low-socioeconomic-status (SES) students. In their study of more than 1,800 students living in poverty, Finn and Rock (1997) found that school engagement was a key factor in whether students stayed in school.

Unfortunately, students are far less engaged than we think (Marks, 2000). In a survey (Yazzie-Mintz, 2007) of 81,000 U.S. high school students, fewer than 2 percent of respondents said that they were never bored. More than 30 percent of respondents claimed that they did not interact with their teachers on a daily basis. An overwhelming 75 percent of respondents said that they were bored because the material they were taught wasn't interesting. Seventy-five percent also indicated that they went to school only to earn a diploma and get out. Not surprisingly, these same students reported spending very little time on homework.

The lack of engagement cited in this study is reflected in other research. Shernoff, Csikszentmihalyi, Schneider, and Shernoff (2003) reported that the average high school student spends over 25 percent of the entire day slumped in his or her chair in a state of apathy. Another study (Pianta, Belsky, Houts, & Morrison, 2007) found that despite students' overwhelming preference for group activities, 5th graders, on average, spent 91 percent of their time either working alone or listening to a teacher, with less than 5 percent of their time spent engaging in group learning activities. In fact, teachers spent over 20 percent of instruction time telling students how to manage materials or time. More critically, children from poverty had only a 10 percent likelihood to experience highly engaging, quality instruction across multiple grades. The authors of this study referred to their findings of the nature and quality of learning opportunities in U.S. elementary classrooms today as "sobering."

These data speak to a significant problem in schools. To get kids to graduate, we need to keep them in school. To keep them in school, we need to make our classrooms relevant, engaging, and full of affirming relationships. If your students are not engaged, it is time to upgrade your skill set and, possibly, your attitudes about students. Students do not magically become more interested and engaged every year they attend school unless *you* get better each year, too.

A Note About Generalizations

The strategies in this book address seven factors that are crucial to student engagement and that are strongly tied to socioeconomic status. In my 2009 book *Teaching with Poverty in Mind,* I cited more than 200 high-quality, peer-reviewed studies showing typical differences between low-SES and high-SES students. I introduced these differences in an attempt to help teachers understand the deep effects of poverty and to bolster their efforts to help students succeed. Some may believe that highlighting the differences between those who grow up poor and those who grow up in middle- or upper-income homes is classist. That is patently false; classism occurs when people promote policies that benefit one class *at the expense* of another.

Of course, it is important to keep in mind that socioeconomic classes are not homogeneous. There are no "average poor people" any more than there are "average middle-class people." A powerful quality of the human brain is to learn from experiences and generalize to aid in subsequent decision making. For example, if you grew up poor and "made it" to the middle class, you might generalize that what worked for you should work for others struggling to advance in socioeconomic status. If the only low-income people you knew were abusing drugs and neglecting their children, you may generalize that poor people are "broken." But it's important to remember that your own world is just a grain of sand on a beach of experiences. Do not assume that your individual experiences are representative of everyone else's. There are loving, joyful families that are poor, just as there are angry, small-minded families that are wealthy.

That said, generalizations are occasionally useful. When the research is compelling, I do generalize. I intend these generalizations to sketch a broad picture of what goes on inside the lives of people living in poverty. Although acknowledging the differences between low-SES and high-SES students may be uncomfortable, we need to accept the fact that there are relevant differences among our students. Understanding this background and the behaviors that stem from it will help you better engage low-SES students in the classroom. If all teachers needed to do to succeed with students who live in poverty was to use the same strategies they already use with middle- and upper-income students, there would be far less of an achievement gap. Instead of fixating on politics or semantics, we need to stay focused on the goal of helping kids graduate and become productive citizens.

Time for a Change

We need to face reality: the same old mind-sets and strategies are not work-ing. It's time for a change. Over the years, I have visited numerous schools with high-poverty populations. Many of you work in schools like these, under difficult circumstances, and I empathize with you. But when you share your problems with me, my response will always be, "So what are you going to do differently tomorrow?" Every day, staff members at high-poverty schools around the world continue to do the same thing and vainly hope for a miracle that will never come. We have to make our own miracles.

In a recent e-mail to me, a principal wrote, "We did a book study on *Teaching with Poverty in Mind,* and our scores are still the same. What hap-pened?" If boosting student achievement were as easy as reading a book, every student's scores would be through the roof. It takes sustained com-mitment to ensure that every student succeeds. Until you make your school the best part of a student's day, you will struggle with student attendance, achievement, and graduation rates. Having a high-achieving school is no accident. It is the result of purposeful, engaged teaching over time.

That's where this book comes in. In *Teaching with Poverty in Mind,* I advocated student engagement as a core strategy to help students of low socioeconomic status succeed, but I had limited space to delve deep into engagement strategies. The purpose of this book is to fill in the gaps—to provide the rationale behind engagement, generate more ideas, and build the attitudes to succeed with students who live in poverty. This book is a "no excuses" resource that will get you on the path toward making good things happen every single day. If students do not come up and thank you for a great class, this book is for you.

Let's walk through how this book can help change the lives of everyone in your school, staff members and students alike.

An Overview of the Book

Chapters 1 and 2 of this book lay the groundwork of the strategies that follow. Chapter 1 reveals seven factors that are crucial to student engagement and that are strongly tied to socioeconomic status. These engagement factors form the rationale behind the specific strategies I advocate and discuss throughout the book. Chapter 2 shares the rules for engagement that teachers are usually never taught but that are essential for success.

Chapters 3 through 7 get into the nitty-gritty of engaging students. Chapter 3 explains how to create a high-energy, engaging, and positive class climate that fosters success every day. Chapter 4 focuses on building cognitive capacity through engagement. Chapter 5 shows you how to build excitement for greater student motivation and effort. Chapter 6 focuses on ways to build a deep, sustained understanding of the content in students' brains. Chapter 7 provides engagement strategies to elevate both energy and focus in your classroom.

Chapters 8 and 9 take a broader view. Chapter 8 empowers you with strategies to automate engagement in your classroom and school, and Chapter 9 prompts you to look forward and plan how you will implement the actions laid out in this book.

An important note: although the first two chapters of this book focus intensely on the seven engagement factors and why the engagement strategies in this book are especially crucial for low-SES students, the remaining chapters often discuss engagement in broader terms. They do not explain in depth how each strategy helps students who live in poverty. This is intentional. Although this book is titled *Engaging Students with Poverty in Mind,* it could just as easily be titled *An Expert Teacher's Guide to Mastering Engagement.* The mind-sets and the strategies in this book will work for every single student—rich, middle-income, or poor—and they can be used by teachers across all grade levels and content areas. As my description of my childhood in the Preface indicates, not all students who grow up in adverse circumstances or are disengaged with school are poor. *If you teach, you will find something that applies to you and your work in this book.* It's just that this book will give you an even greater return on your investment with students who live in poverty.

Experiencing adverse circumstances as a child can shape a person's entire life. I know this personally, and maybe you do, too. This book is in your hands because engagement is the crucial factor that combats these circumstances and helps keep kids in school and on the path toward success.

This book has been a joy to write, and I hope you find it a joy to read and implement. Let's all work together to make both your work and your school *way* more engaging. When we do, everybody will win. Are you game?

1

The Seven Engagement Factors

During the last 75 years, engaging low-SES students has been a challenge to public and private school teachers alike. Although most teachers have traditionally succeeded in reaching students who come from middle- and upper-income homes, they struggle to reach economically disadvantaged students.

This engagement gap is often blamed on ineffective local, state, and federal policies. It is widely acknowledged that poor students are more likely to attend schools that receive inadequate funding (Carey, 2005), pay lower teacher salaries (Karoly, 2001), have larger class sizes, provide a less rigorous curriculum, retain fewer experienced teachers (Barton, 2005), and are less likely to be safe learning environments.

But if these factors are so compelling, how do we explain the success stories? There is a key bit of evidence missing from this litany of adverse factors: over 50 percent of the academic outcomes of school-age children stem not from public policy but from what the teacher does in the classroom (Hattie, 2008). *Teaching matters more than any other factor in a student's school years.* In fact, research (Hanushek, 2005) tells us that quality teaching can completely offset the devastating effects poverty has on students' academic performance. Here's how: if any teacher performs at one standard deviation in quality (as measured by student achievement) above the district's mean adequate yearly progress rate for five years in a row, the resulting improvement in student learning would *entirely close the gap* between the performance of a typical student from poverty and the performance of a higher-income student. If you are serious about helping kids succeed, stop wishing for a miracle. Five years of strong teaching *is* the miracle.

Although it may be understandable to complain about the "system" or local politics, these complaints do not amount to a valid excuse. With so many Title I schools succeeding, blaming the system is hollow reasoning. Nobody is buying into the excuses anymore.

It is time to end our pattern of failure. But before we tackle solutions, it will be helpful to gain an understanding of *why* so many teachers have difficulty working with and graduating students who live in poverty.

The Seven Engagement Factors

In my broad survey of the research and through my many years of experience, I have uncovered seven factors that correlate with student engagement and that are strongly tied to socioeconomic status:

The Seven Engagement Factors
1. Health and nutrition
2. Vocabulary
3. Effort and energy
4. Mind-set
5. Cognitive capacity
6. Relationships
7. Stress level

How can we decide which factors are more significant than others? In addition to my own findings, there is a standardized scale that measures the relative size of an intervention or factor known as *effect size*. The effect size is particularly useful for quantifying effects from widely varying scales and for understanding the comparative influence of each. Throughout this book, I occasionally touch on an engagement factor or strategy's effect size as a way of showing its degree of impact. Generally, an effect size falls into one of five groups: negative, marginal, positive, substantial, or enormous (see Figure 1.1).

Figure 1.1   Understanding Effect Size

Under 0.00 = negative effect
0.00–0.20 = marginal effect
0.20–0.40 = positive effect
0.40–0.60 = substantial effect
0.60–2.00 = enormous effect

Let's review the research background of each of the seven key factors and its connection to socioeconomic status and student engagement. You'll see that growing up in poverty can affect students in wide-ranging ways that may surprise you.

Factor 1: Health and Nutrition

Physical, mental, and emotional health support engagement and learning. Sadly, the lower a child's socioeconomic status is, the greater the health risks he or she faces (Sapolsky, 2005). The lower parents' income is, the more likely it is that children will be born premature, low in birth weight, or with disabilities (Bradley & Corwyn, 2002). Compared with their higher-SES counterparts, people living in poverty are less likely to exercise, get proper diagnoses of health problems, receive appropriate and prompt medical attention, or be prescribed appropriate medications or interventions (Evans, Wells, & Moch, 2003). They experience a higher incidence of such conditions as asthma (Gottlieb, Beiser, & O'Connor, 1995), untreated ear infections and hearing-loss issues (Menyuk, 1980), tuberculosis (Rogers & Ginzberg, 1993), and obesity (Wang & Zhang, 2006). In addition, people living in poverty are more likely to live in old and inadequately maintained homes with peeling paint and outdated plumbing, which increases their exposure to lead (Sargent et al., 1995), and their neighborhoods are less likely to provide high-quality social, municipal, and local services (Evans, 2004). A study of 3,000 subjects found that low-SES people are also more likely to have mental health problems (Xue, Leventhal, Brooks-Gunn, & Earls, 2005).

Each of these health-related factors has a significant effect on cognition and behavior. For example, exposure to lead correlates with poor working memory and a weaker ability to link cause and effect. That means that although your students may know the behavior rules, they won't necessarily understand when and how those rules apply. Students with ear infections may have additional trouble with sound discrimination, making it tough for them to follow directions, engage in demanding auditory processing, or even understand the teacher.

Many of the health problems experienced by lower-SES people can be linked to poor nutrition. In 2010, 14.5 percent of U.S. families were food insecure (Coleman-Jensen, Nord, Andrews, & Carlson, 2011). Skipping breakfast is disproportionately prevalent among urban minority youth, many of whom live in poverty. Recent research suggests it has had a clear negative impact on their academic achievement by adversely affecting cognition and absenteeism (Basch, 2011).

In addition to inadequate *quantity* of food, food *quality* is also an issue: children who are raised in poor households typically eat a low-cost, low-nutrition diet that can have adverse effects on the brain (Gómez-Pinilla, 2008).

Poor nutrition poses a strong risk to students' learning and engagement. When kids don't eat well, or when they don't eat at all, their behavior suffers, and they have a tougher time learning. Poor nutrition at breakfast affects gray-matter mass in kids' brains (Taki, 2010). Deficiencies in minerals are linked to weaker memory, and low levels of certain nutrients such as omega-3 fatty acids are linked to depression.

The two most important fuels for the brain are oxygen and glucose. To get a stable supply of glucose to the brain, kids ideally should eat either a high-protein breakfast including, for example, lean meats, eggs, or yogurt, or one that includes complex carbohydrates, such as oatmeal. Either of these breakfasts will stabilize and manage the levels of glucose over several hours. In contrast, simple carbohydrates such as sugary cereals, pastries, PopTarts, pancakes, or fast food—which are often what poor children eat for breakfast—create wide fluctuations in blood sugar. Unstable glucose levels, whether too high or too low, are linked to weaker cognitive and behavioral outcomes (Wang, Szabo, & Dykman, 2004).

Although hunger does have an adverse effect on academic performance, food quality is more important than quantity (Weinreb et al., 2002).

Cognitively, it's better to eat less but better-quality food. The brain actually produces more new brain cells on a restricted-calorie diet than on an ordinary one (Kitamura, Mishina, & Sugiyama, 2006).

Although the factor of health and nutrition is the least directly addressed engagement factor in this book and is not easily "fixed" by teachers, I include it because it strongly affects most of the other six engagement factors. Poor health and nutrition cannot be ignored; nor should they be used as an excuse for letting students underperform. Before you assume that poor nutrition is the irreparable cause of your students' unsatisfactory behavior or academic performance, consider this: thousands of teachers succeed with low-SES students who don't have ideal diets but who nevertheless demonstrate appropriate behavior and earn high achievement scores. You have a greater effect on your students' performance than you may think. Creating a highly engaging classroom can help compensate for behavioral and cognitive issues resulting from poor nutrition. Chapter 7 discusses strategies you can use to help regulate students' glucose and oxygen levels.

Factor 2: Vocabulary

A child's vocabulary is part of his or her brain's toolkit for learning, memory, and cognition. Words help children represent, manipulate, and reframe information. Unfortunately, the vocabulary differences among children of different socioeconomic status are staggering. A six-year study by Hart and Risley (2003) found that by age 3, the children of professional parents were adding words to their vocabularies at about twice the rate of children in welfare families. Both the quantity and the quality of phrases directed at the children by caregivers correlated directly with income levels. Here's another stunning illustration of the vocabulary chasm: *toddlers* from middle- and upper-income families actually used more words in talking to their parents than low-SES *mothers* used in talking to their own children (Bracey, 2006).

Low-SES students' smaller vocabularies place them at risk for academic failure (Gonzalez, 2005; Hoff, 2003; Walker, Greenwood, Hart, & Carta, 1994). It's up to teachers to try to build low-SES students' vocabularies. Otherwise, these students will struggle and disengage. When students don't understand many of the words used in class or in their reading materials, they may tune out or believe that school is not for them. Often, they won't participate because they don't want to risk looking stupid, especially in front of their peers.

Vocabulary building *must* form a key part of the enrichment experiences for students at school. Academic vocabulary—the vocabulary students need in order to understand the concepts and content taught in the various subject areas and to succeed on tests—is particularly critical. Teachers must be relentless about using nonverbal communication, visual aids, and context to add meaning and incorporate vocabulary building in engagement activities whenever appropriate.

Factor 3: Effort and Energy

The sight of kids slouching in their chairs, inattentive to the goings-on of the class, is a familiar one to many teachers. But uninformed teachers often interpret the reasons behind the disengagement differently according to SES. Whereas they may label middle-income students as "not reaching their potential," they often assume that low-income students are simply lazy, or that they show little effort because their parents are lazy.

Yet people living in poverty typically value education as much as middle-income people do (Compton-Lilly, 2003), and they spend at least as many hours working each week as do their higher-SES counterparts (Bernstein, Mishel, & Boushey, 2002). In fact, almost two-thirds of low-income families include at least one parent who works full-time and year-round (Gorski, 2008). There is no "inherited laziness" passed down from poor parents to their children. Poor people simply work at lower-paying jobs.

Students living in poverty are practical about what motivates them. They want to know who the teacher really is, and they want the teaching to connect to their world. When teachers cannot or will not connect personally, students are less likely to trust them. Teachers must make connections to low-SES students' culture in ways that help the students see a viable reason to play the academic "game." When teachers remain ignorant of their students' culture, students often experience a demotivating disconnect between the school world and their home life (Lindsey, Karns, & Myatt, 2010). As a result, they give up. Who you are and how you teach both have a huge influence on whether low-SES students will bother to engage.

Effort matters a great deal in learning. If you see motivational differences in the classroom, remember your own school days. When you were affirmed, challenged, and encouraged, you worked harder. When the learning got you excited, curious, and intrigued, you put in more effort. We've all seen how students will often work much harder in one class than in another. The difference is in the teaching. When you care about your students, they respond. When kids like and respect you, they try harder.

A student who is not putting in effort is essentially telling you that your teaching is not engaging. Give that same kid an engaging teacher, and a whole new student will emerge. The teacher has the power to make a difference. Take control and be the determining factor in the classroom.

Factor 4: Mind-Set

Research suggests that lower socioeconomic status often correlates with a negative view of the future (Robb, Simon, & Wardle, 2009) and a sense of helplessness. Positive response outcome expectancy ("coping") is associated with high subjective SES, whereas no expectancy ("helplessness") is associated with low subjective SES (Odéen et al., 2013). In short, poverty is associated with lowered expectations about future outcomes.

When it comes to success in school, mind-set is a crucial internal attitude for both students and teachers. A student's attitude about learning is a moderately robust predictive factor of academic achievement (Blackwell, Trzesniewski, & Dweck, 2007). Taken together, student mind-set and teacher support can form either a significant asset or a serious liability. When both teachers and students believe that students have a fixed amount of "smarts" that cannot be increased, students are far more likely to disengage. Conversely, when students have positive attitudes about their own learning capacity, and when teachers focus on growth and change rather than on having students reach arbitrary milestones—a strategy that leaves students more vulnerable to negative feedback and thus more likely to disengage from challenging learning opportunities (Mangels, Butterfield, Lamb, Good, & Dweck, 2006)—student engagement increases.

Often, teachers underestimate the prevalence of negative emotions in their students' lives (Jordan et al., 2011) and misinterpret these emotions. For example, they may view anger as a sign of students' insubordination or lack of self-control, when it is more likely to be a symptom of depression. Teachers may unknowingly reinforce false assumptions that certain students don't have the "mental strength" or "staying power" to succeed, and that belief can hurt students' performance (Miller et al., 2012) and substantially affect students' ability to recruit their cognitive resources to sustain learning over time.

Therefore, teacher support is essential to the academic success of low-SES students, many of whom do not believe in their capacity to learn and grow. Teachers' positive, growth-oriented mind-sets can help compensate for students' negative mind-sets. Gradually, with teacher support, students will begin to believe in themselves and in their capacity to reach their goals and thus increase their own learning success.

Factor 5: Cognitive Capacity

Cognitive capacity is highly complex. It can be measured in many different ways and is affected significantly by socioeconomic status. Socioeconomic status is strongly associated with a number of measures of cognitive ability, including IQ, achievement tests, grade retention rates, and literacy (Baydar, Brooks-Gunn, & Furstenberg, 1993; Brooks-Gunn, Guo, & Furstenberg, 1993; Liaw & Brooks-Gunn, 1994; Smith, Brooks-Gunn, & Klebanov, 1997). Studies show that low-SES children perform below higher-SES children on tests of intelligence and academic achievement (Bradley & Corwyn, 2002; Duncan, Brooks-Gunn, & Klebanov, 1994) and are also more likely to fail courses, be placed in special education, or drop out of high school (McLoyd, 1998).

Poverty affects the physical brain. In poor children's brains, the hippocampus—the critical structure for new learning and memory—is smaller, with less volume (Hanson, Chandra, Wolfe, & Pollak, 2011). A 2008 study (Amat et al.) showed a correlation between hippocampal volume and general intelligence.

Adverse environmental factors can artificially suppress children's IQ. For example, poor children are more likely to be exposed to lead, which correlates with poor working memory. The majority of children with low working memory struggle in both learning measures and verbal ability and exhibit such cognitive problems as short attention spans, high levels of distractibility, problems in monitoring the quality of their work, and difficulties in generating new solutions to problems (Alloway, Gathercole, Kirkwood, & Elliott, 2009).

The good news is that a brain that is susceptible to adverse environmental effects is equally susceptible to positive, enriching effects. IQ is not fixed, and we can influence many of the factors affecting it. Students with low cognitive capacity are ripe for an engaging teacher who is willing to teach the core cognitive skills that lead to academic success.

Factor 6: Relationships

All children need reliable, positive adults in their lives. When a child's early experiences are chaotic, or if at least one parent is absent, the child's developing brain often becomes insecure and stressed. This insecurity is more pronounced among children living in poverty. Marriage rates have dropped by half in the last two generations among low-SES populations (Fields, 2004). Almost three-fourths of all poor parents with children are unmarried, compared with about one-fourth of higher-SES parents (Bishaw & Renwick, 2009).

Strong and secure home relationships help support and stabilize children's behavior. Children who grow up with positive relationships learn healthy, appropriate emotional responses to everyday situations. Children raised in poor households often fail to learn these responses because of absent or stressed caregivers. Learning these responses requires countless hours of positive caregiving (Malatesta & Izard, 1984), which poor children are less likely to receive than their higher-SES peers. In poor homes, the ratio of positives (affirmations) to negatives (reprimands) is typically a 1-to-2 ratio. Contrast this to the 6-to-1 positives-to-negatives ratio in the homes of higher-income families (Hart & Risley, 1995).

These relational deficits can negatively affect students' engagement and achievement. The probability of dropout and school failure increases as a function of the timing and length of time children were exposed to relational adversity (Spilt, Hughes, Wu, & Kwok, 2012). Poor emotional regulation among prekindergarten children predicts academic difficulties in 1st grade (Trentacosta & Izard, 2007). Low-SES adolescents are more likely to experience depression (Tomarken, Dichter, Garber, & Simien, 2004), and among older students, lower SES is associated with overreacting to others' emotions (Gianaros et al., 2008), which can lead to inappropriate school behaviors. Social dysfunction may inhibit students' ability to work well in cooperative groups. This exclusion can hurt overall classroom cooperation and harmony and lead to increasingly troubled academic performance and behavior.

Many poor children simply do not have the repertoire of necessary social-emotional responses for school. It is easy to misinterpret low-SES students' emotional and social differences as a lack of respect, poor manners, or laziness. Yet it is more accurate and helpful to understand that many poor students come to school with a narrower-than-expected range of appropriate emotional responses. Many simply do not know how to behave.

Developing strong teacher-student relationships helps counter the negative effects of these inappropriate emotional responses and has a profound effect on student engagement. To succeed, you may need to shift your own responses. Instead of disciplining students for poor emotional responsiveness, teach them how to respond in ways that will help keep them out of trouble. Instead of becoming upset, retool your thinking, open your heart, and show students how to behave. Learn to reframe your thinking: *expect* that students may be impulsive, blurt inappropriate language, and act "disrespectful" until you teach them otherwise. *Expect* kids to test their boundaries until they learn stronger social and emotional skills. They will exhibit coarse behavior until the relationships you build and the school's social conditions make it attractive for them *not* to behave inappropriately.

Factor 7: Stress Level

Stress can be defined as the body's response to the perception of loss of control resulting from an adverse situation or person. Small amounts of stress are healthy; in fact, occasional stress can actually build resilience. However, children raised in poverty are more likely than their affluent peers to experience both acute and chronic stress (Almeida, Neupert, Banks, & Serido, 2005; Evans & Schamberg, 2009), which leave a devastating imprint on their lives. *Acute stress* refers to severe, intense stress resulting from exposure to such trauma as abuse or violence, whereas *chronic stress* refers to high stress sustained over time.

The frequency and intensity of both stressful life events and daily hassles are greater among low-SES children (Attar, Guerra, & Tolan, 1994). In any given year, more than half of all poor children deal with evictions, utility disconnections, overcrowding, or lack of a stove or refrigerator, compared with only 13 percent of well-off children (Lichter, 1997). In addition, compared with middle-income children, low-SES children are exposed to higher levels of familial violence, disruption, and separation (Emery & Laumann-Billings, 1998). Abuse is a major stressor. Caregivers' disciplinary measures grow harsher as income decreases (Gershoff, 2002; Slack, Holl, McDaniel, Yoo, & Bolger, 2004). Lower-income parents tend to be more authoritarian with their children, issuing harsh demands and inflicting physical punishment (Bradley, Corwyn, Burchinal, McAdoo, & Coll, 2001).

Stress exerts a relentless, insidious influence on children's physical, psychological, emotional, and cognitive functioning—areas that affect brain development, academic success, and social competence (Evans, Kim, Ting, Tesher, & Shannis, 2007). At school, a child who comes from a stressful home environment tends to channel that stress into disruptive behavior (Bradley & Corwyn, 2002), such as impulsivity. Impulsivity is commonly misdiagnosed as AD/HD, but it is actually an exaggerated response to stress that serves as a survival mechanism: in conditions of poverty, those most likely to survive are those who have an exaggerated stress response. Each risk factor in a student's life increases impulsivity and diminishes his or her capacity to defer gratification (Evans, 2003).

Acute stress in particular is more likely to lead to aggressive, "in-your-face" behavior. In the context of a high-stress life, aggression enables a student to feel in control and take charge of a situation. Like impulsivity, it's an exaggerated stress response that serves as a survival strategy: fight first, ask questions later. Aggressive school behaviors include talking back to the teacher, getting in the teacher's face, or showing inappropriate body language or facial responses.

Conversely, chronic stress can result in the opposite effect: an increased sense of detachment and hopelessness over time (Bolland, Lian, & Formichella, 2005). Low-SES students are more likely to give up or become passive and uninterested in school (Johnson, 1981). This giving-up process is known as *learned helplessness* (Hiroto & Seligman, 1975) and, sadly, frequently takes hold as early as 1st grade. The more stress children experience, the more they perceive events as uncontrollable and unpredictable—and the less hope they feel about making changes in their lives (Henry, 2005). Passive school behaviors include failure to respond to questions or requests, passivity, slumped posture, and disconnection from peers or academics.

All of these behaviors—both aggressive and passive—are often interpreted as being signs of "an attitude" or laziness, but they are actually symptoms of stress disorders. Overall, stress has an insidious effect on student engagement. It is linked to more than 50 percent of all absences (Johnston-Brooks, Lewis, Evans, & Whalen, 1998); impairs attention and concentration (Erickson, Drevets, & Schulkin, 2003); reduces motivation and effort (Johnson, 1981); and increases the likelihood of depression (Hammack, Robinson, Crawford, & Li, 2004).

But kids are not stuck this way. For example, when aggressive low-SES students attended classes that taught appropriate coping skills and stress-relieving techniques, there was a decrease in hostility (Wadsworth, Raviv, Compas, & Connor-Smith, 2005). Similarly, giving students appropriate amounts of control over their daily lives at school helps diminish the effects of chronic and acute stress and increases engagement. Later in the book, we will explore why giving students more control over their classroom experiences is part of the solution (Kraus, Piff, & Keltner, 2009).

Making a Difference

In the following chapters, you will learn powerful engagement strategies that will help you nurture a positive climate, build cognitive capacity, encourage greater effort, build understanding, and activate energy. Starting with Chapter 3, each chapter includes a section at the beginning called "The

Connecting Engagement Factors." This section lists which of the seven key engagement factors connect with the strategies provided in the chapter. Some chapters will connect to more factors than others, but the book as a whole will enable you to influence every single one of the seven engagement factors discussed here. It's not easy: this process requires you to upgrade your repertoire, roll up your sleeves, get a fiercely positive attitude, and charge ahead into your job. But you can make a difference.

2

The Rules for Engagement

In the Classroom

Larisa taught a combined 4th and 5th grade class in her Title I school. Now in her third year as a teacher, she was feeling discouraged. As she often did, she vented in the lunchroom: "I know my principal wants more student engagement. But these kids just sit there. I use the same activities that other, more experienced teachers say are good ones, but they just don't work on the kids I have. I'm doing the right things, but the kids are not engaged. This sucks."

Tammy, sitting two tables away, overheard. Most days, the noises from other teachers went in one ear and out the other, but today, Tammy thought it was time to do something. She went over to Larisa and asked, "Can I sit here for a moment?" Once she got the nod, she sat down and faced Larisa. "I've been in your shoes. You sound like me when I started teaching. I used to get so frustrated. The problem was always the curriculum, the activities, or the kids."

Larisa asked, "You mean it has nothing to do with those things?"

"Yes and no," Tammy responded. "I discovered that it has much more to do with me than I thought. Today, kids in my class are so much more engaged than they used to be years ago. And the kids haven't changed; it's me that's different."

"So how did you change?" Larisa asked.

"Well, I decided to figure out how things worked. There were attitudes I needed to adopt, rules I needed to learn, and, frankly, a lot of changes I needed to make."

Larisa, normally chatty, was quiet. The wheels began turning in her brain. *Maybe it's time for a new start,* she thought.

The Five Rules for Engagement

When I was a novice teacher, I was always on the lookout for the next big strategy to use in class. Unfortunately, the outcomes of my activities had a checkered report card. Some things worked, and some didn't. It was easy to blame the curriculum (boring), the activities (flawed), or the kids (disengaged). But day after day and year after year, the curriculum changed, the activities changed, and the kids changed. There was only one common denominator over the years: me. It was time to hold up a mirror to my own practice.

Have you ever noticed that some teachers will find a way to struggle with even the most solid strategy, while other teachers can somehow make a weak strategy work spectacularly well? The difference lies in the extent to which teachers follow the implicit rules for engagement that guide success. Just as soldiers need to know their rules of engagement before going on a mission, teachers need rules for engagement to complete their own mission of helping students succeed.

Here's a common scenario: a teacher goes to a conference and sees an engagement strategy modeled. He decides to use it in his own classroom. Unfortunately, it doesn't reap results. The teacher decides that the strategy does not work on "certain students," or that it's just a bad strategy. Time for the next one!

The teacher in this scenario resembles the romantic searching for his ideal match and, throughout that search, discarding potential partners, date after date after date. At some point, the searcher realizes, "Maybe *I* have something to do with this inability to find what I want!" In the case of the teacher, he never followed the rules that would enable him to make the strategy work every time.

Good teachers internalize these rules, and good teachers matter more than curriculum, the administration, or what students eat for breakfast (Hattie, 2008). Yes, those factors do have an impact on student engagement and achievement, but their role doesn't come close to the role that good teaching plays.

You can accomplish your mission of high achievement, but you won't randomly stumble into success. If you work at a high-poverty school, you have even less room for error. This chapter reveals the five core rules for engagement—unwritten rules until now—that will help you build a foundation for success. Read them closely, internalize them, and incorporate them into your practice. These rules power the rest of the strategies in this book—indeed, *any* strategies—and following them will make your instruction flow better, improve student behavior and learning, and even make your life a bit easier.

The Five Rules for Engagement

1. Upgrade your attitude.
2. Build relationships and respect.
3. Get buy-in.
4. Embrace clarity.
5. Show your passion.

Rule #1: Upgrade Your Attitude

The classic Patti Labelle song "New Attitude" has it right: now that the singer has a new attitude, she finally knows where she's going and what to do. You, too, can turn things around by embracing a new, positive attitude. How often have you thought, *I hope I get a good batch of kids this year*? Upgrade your attitude and think instead, *I know the kids I get are going to love the new engagement strategies I'll be using this year.* Students keenly sense teachers' attitudes toward them, so a positive, optimistic attitude is crucial.

Engagement is about both attitude and strategy. Make the decision to engage every student every day. When you survey your class, do not let a sea of blank faces discourage you. This book will show you how to engage students powerfully and consistently, even on rough days. As Chapter 1 discussed, when teachers hold negative beliefs about their students, they not only undermine student engagement but also hurt students' performance. Low-SES students in particular need you to believe in them so that they can believe in themselves.

Solutions You Can Use

Use affirmations. Write out a simple affirmation like "I choose to engage every student, every day of the week." Post it somewhere you'll see it, and read it daily. Affirm students, too. Affirm them for showing up on time, for being seated on time, and for contributing in class.

Employ occasional small engagers. When kids feel fatigued or low on energy, their attitudes get bogged down, too. Use small engaging activities that keep the class moving. Ask students to stand and stretch. Ask them to identify something they just learned by pointing to the appropriate wall poster. Ask them to take in a slow deep breath of confidence, hold it, and then slowly exhale all their stress. Use simple social activities that have students pair up to solve a problem or complete a posted quiz.

Give yourself permission to fail. Always have a backup plan for what to do or say when something doesn't work (e.g., "Oops! Class, we'll get that right next time. Let's move on to another activity"). Just keep a log or make a mental note of what worked and what didn't. Nobody got good at engagement overnight. Forgive yourself, remember your mistakes, and keep learning. Chapter 9 (pp. 169–172) addresses in greater depth what to do when a strategy or approach fails.

Rule #2: Build Relationships and Respect

A critical step in creating an engaging classroom is to build relationships and respect. Remember this aphorism: *students don't care how much you know until they know how much you care.* Students who have positive relationships with their teachers experience less stress, behave more appropriately, and feel more excited about learning. Students almost always work harder for teachers they like (Cornelius-White & Harbaugh, 2010). Hamre and

Pianta (2001) found that strong student-teacher relationships in kindergarten had robust effects on students' school outcomes that lasted through 8th grade. Keeping in mind that, as Figure 1.1 (p. 9) showed, any effect size over 0.40 is substantial, consider this: teacher-student relationships have a whopping 0.72 effect size when it comes to student achievement (Hattie, 2008). Improvements in teacher-student relationship quality are consistently associated with improvements in teacher-reported academic skills and reductions in behavior problems throughout elementary school (Maldonado-Carreño & Votruba-Drzal, 2011).

As a child, I experienced significant instability. After living with three different stepmothers, my biggest wish was for stable parents who cared. The two teachers who did care made a lifelong impact on me. Although relationships matter to all students, students with less-stable home lives have a particular need for strong relationships at school and are more likely to want to connect with you. This is a biological need, not a "frill": researchers (Luby et al., 2012) have found that love and support correlate with increased hippocampus size—the area most responsible for learning, memory, and emotional regulation. The next time you feel hesitant to show caring toward your kids, remember that relationships can affect brain capacity!

Students come to school wondering, "Am I liked? Do I fit in? Does the teacher care about me and my world?" Even if you care a great deal, students may not realize it, so keep in mind that students need to see, hear, and feel the caring. A retiring teacher once told me, "I wish someone had told me how much I meant to my students. I never knew." Make yourself a memo: "I won't know how hard my own students will work for me until I show them how much I care about their lives."

Solutions You Can Use

Share a bit of yourself every day. All it takes to connect is sharing a 60-second vignette about yourself: your family, your dreams, your everyday life. Each week, share at least one story about your life. In addition, find out about your students every day. Learn about their dreams, hobbies, family, neighborhood, problems, and passions. If you don't get to know your students better every day, your odds of success just dropped.

Here's a true story illustrating why this is such an important practice. At the start of a recent school year, an elementary school teacher I know asked her students, "What do you want to do when you grow up?" One student responded, "I wanna be like my daddy and be on welfare." Instead of lowering her standards for a student who obviously had such low expectations for himself, she determined to broaden his horizons. All year long, she shared stories of her own adventures with her class, describing trips and excursions she went on and showing them inspiring pictures. At the end of the school year, she asked the same student what he wanted to be when he grew up. This time, he said, "I wanna be a teacher!"

Respect your students. Even if your students don't particularly like you, you need their respect. Students who respect you know you're a professional who is looking out for their long-term best interests, and they will naturally be more engaged in learning. To earn your students' respect, you must respect them. You don't need to like your students' world, but never disparage or criticize a student's background, heritage, or culture.

You must integrate students' cultural and social capital into any goals or criteria for success you set for them (Putnam, 2000). Getting high grades is not in itself a high priority for many students, so setting academic goals in a meaningful context makes all the difference. For example, if you define students' goal in a writing class as making their voices heard, or in a social studies class as participating in community projects, they are much more likely to engage. Make good grades the by-product of success in your class, not the central goal.

You have the ability to engage every student, every day. But first, students need to believe that you're on their side, not an adversary. When you're planning a lesson, ask yourself, "Does this activity run the risk of making students uncomfortable? Could they be embarrassed if they fail at it?" Students must trust that you won't put them into impossible situations or make fools out of them. You'll gain respect from them by respecting them, respecting yourself, and being fair.

Upgrade your interactive language. During every single interaction with your students, make eye contact and affirm the good in them. Show you value them by using the same language with them that you would want directed toward you. This means always using respectful words and phrases like "please," "thank you," "at your convenience," and "when you have a moment." Never tell students to "knock it off!", "shut up!", or "sit down!" You would not take that kind of abuse yourself, and it has no place in a classroom. Your students are not prison inmates; they are the future of our country, and the reason you have a job.

When you respond to students' questions or answers, do you thank them for their contributions? Do your responses lead them to "gain" or "lose" in the eyes of their peers? Do you treat every student as a competent human being with a future that might change lives? Do you put students down or honor their dreams?

Rule #3: Get Buy-In

One of the most critical skills teachers can learn is never taught to them. This skill is salesmanship.

For many students, school is an obligation, not a joy and a privilege. This means you need to "sell" the learning to them. When you step into the classroom of a high-performing teacher, several things will likely jump out at you. The first is that the teacher is so strongly committed to engaging students that there's a palpable "whatever it takes" attitude in the air. Passionate, committed teachers do not accept failure as an option. They are constantly "selling" students on themselves, the content, and the learning process. Student motivation counts for a strong 0.48 effect size toward student achievement (Hattie, 2008). Highly effective teachers raise their odds of success by ensuring that students *want* to participate, *will* engage, and *choose* to learn. The results speak for themselves.

Any given school day is full of hundreds of micro-events. People talk, situations develop, and students act and react. Most of the day's energy is simply noise to the brain. If students don't find content relevant, or if they don't believe they need to know it, they will often pull the plug on the learning and disconnect.

If you're thinking that it is *students'* responsibility to engage, look at it this way: in a national survey (Yazzie-Mintz, 2007) of 81,000 high school students, two of three said that the only reason they were in school was because their friends were there, and more than half responded, "Because it's the law!" Being ordered around by teachers and having no choice in their learning can be rough on students. Most of them have enough issues just trying to grow up. Appreciate students' point of view, and don't blame them for complacency; many have been conditioned by years of boredom and compliance *not* to engage. You'll need to figure out how to get students to buy into what you're doing, or they won't engage at all. Getting buy-in is closely connected to another of the five rules for engagement: build relationships and respect. When you respect students and build positive relationships, they will be much more receptive to what you're selling.

The best strategy to get buy-in is to create a hook that pulls in students enough to at least try the next step. Often, once the task begins—if it's relevant, challenging, and well paced—it will provide its own motivation. Here are some hooks to consider using with your own students.

Solutions You Can Use

Issue the "bigger kid" challenge. Intrigue students by saying, "Here's something we usually save for next year," or "I know you're in 2nd grade now, but let's try out something that usually only 3rd graders can do." Pique secondary students' interest by issuing a challenge: "I'm not sure if you can do this or not, but let's give it a try."

Offer an incentive. Use an incentive to get buy-in: "Hey, if we finish this up on time, we'll have enough time left for our favorite story." Or give students an offer they can't refuse: "How many of you would like to learn something new, make a friend, and still finish up early?" With secondary students, try making a deal: "Listen, I could use some help. I'll trade you a free homework pass for your help on this."

Pique students' curiosity. Start a lesson by holding up a mystery box and telling students, "You can ask me three questions about the contents of this box." You might also kick off a lesson using relevant props with an "edge"— unusual or strange things that drip, make sounds, or are even alive. Intrigue elementary students by asking, "Can I share a secret with you?" Pull in secondary students with a little risk and edginess: "I really should not be telling you this," or "I don't know if anyone's done this experiment before; it might not work. Are you willing to give it a try?"

Start a competition. Have students compete with themselves ("Look at this chart to see how you did last week. I am guessing you can do even better this week"). They can also compete with one another ("We'll work in small teams and see which one gets the solution first"). For older students, succeeding in competition can build status. Sweeten the deal with a reward: "The team that gets all of these questions right gets one free homework pass next week."

Chunk down the buy-in. Stair-step an activity by saying, "Everyone, stand up and slide your chair in. Now take seven steps and find a partner. Introduce yourself. Share two foods that gross you out. Now decide who goes first. Great! The one who goes first gets to ask the next question posted up front." Notice that you never actually tell students up front what the activity is; you simply let them tiptoe into it with fun pre-steps. Another "trick" is the missing-piece activity. Have students find partners, then give each pair two minutes to solve a math problem that is missing one part. When students aren't able to solve the problem, they understand why that part is so critical and actually want the missing piece.

Lower the stakes. You're more likely to hook students when you occasionally lower the stakes. Students afraid of failure or embarrassment are less likely to lose their inhibitions and fully immerse themselves in the lesson. You could preface an activity by saying, "Usually this assignment is given for homework, but today we're simply going to review it for possible use for next year's students. Let's break it down, and each team will work on a different section." Consider also reframing mistakes by making failure a part of the learning process. This reframing helps students revise negative internal narratives. Call on students who are sure they have wrong answers. If they can tell you what they did wrong and explain how they'll do it differently next time, they get a privilege or free homework pass.

Use their imagination. Draw in younger students using the power of pretend. For example, start an activity or a lesson with a hypothetical situation: "Let's pretend we need four friends for a party," or "Think of a famous person. If you were that person, how would you do this?" Have secondary students make predictions: "How do you think this will turn out? Go ahead and tell your neighbor your guess. Now write it down, so we can come back to it later."

Rule #4: Embrace Clarity

To become extraordinary at engagement, you need to master the details that make up the big picture. According to research (Chesebro, 2003), the clarity of teachers' words and actions is strongly linked to student engagement. Word choice correlates positively with student comprehension of material (Myers & Knox, 2001) and influences what students learn from their teachers (Ginsberg, 2007). A study of college students found that student persistence correlated with the clarity of instruction they received (Pascarella, Salisbury, & Blaich, 2009). With a staggering effect size of 0.75, teacher clarity ranks in the top 10 of all student achievement factors (Hattie, 2008). There are several keys to achieving clarity.

Preparation is essential. Before using an engagement strategy, you should know its purpose, the content or skills it will cover, and its parameters (e.g., length of time required, degree of social interaction, materials needed, and directions for students). Plan with purpose, and think through the lesson from the student's point of view. A lesson-planning website like my own 10-Minute Lesson Plans (www.10minutelessonplans.com) can help you build structured, thoughtful, research-based lesson plans that you can e-mail, print, or save for future use.

Solutions You Can Use

Use fewer words. When what you're saying is important, speak with intention, and pause instead of adding more words. Find a metaphor or an analogy that saves 100 words. For example, in a biology class, you can introduce the brain's hippocampus by explaining that it works like a surge protector. Let your body language do the heavy lifting. If you want students to put *their* hands up, put *yours* up. Walk to a different area of the classroom when the content you're discussing needs a new reference point. Consider replacing a verbal explanation of the lesson's content or process with a visual or manipulatives.

Say what you do want from students, not what you don't want. Telling students what *not* to do not only places the focus on the negative (which is never constructive) but also fails to cultivate the change you want. In contrast, focusing on positive, desired behavior actually helps shape students' future success. Here are some examples of poorly phrased requests and positive alternatives you can use:

- Replace "I need your eyes up front" with "Eyes up front, please. You'll need to know this later." Don't beg or plead; simply state what you want and why.

- Replace "Don't look out the window" with "Watch this carefully. Here's why it's important."

- Replace "I want you to pay attention" with "Focus on this object for a second, please."

- Replace "I need all of you to have a seat, *now*!" with "When you're ready to learn something new, have a seat." Those who remain standing will sit down after finding that they didn't get a rise out of you and that their friends are bored with their act. Be patient, and let them decide when to take a seat. As your relationships improve, students' behavior will improve.

- Replace "Tim, I need you to take your foot off of Kim's chair and put it down on the floor" with "Looks like a good time for a quick stretch. Please stand up." Avoid public, status-costing (for the student) power struggles, and do not exert your authority over a minor instance of misbehavior. The student is propping up his foot because your class is low on energy and he's bored. Read the signs and learn when students are telling you that it's time to get up for a stretch.

Give clear, simple directions. The more you try to explain an activity, the more time you give students to wonder why you are justifying it. Keep it simple, and focus on your students' world, not yours. Use landmarks and objects as reference points rather than relative directions. For example, say, "Look toward the window, then toward the clock" rather than "Look left, then right." The following steps—which I advise you to use as a general framework, not a rigid formula—will help you achieve consistency and precision. This particular example is for a think-pair-share activity.

1. Use a quick hook to attract attention and get buy-in. ("Hey, I've got a great idea!")

2. Tell them when they will start the activity, but never go longer than 30 seconds. ("In just 10 seconds . . .")

3. Use a consistent trigger word. ("When I say 'Go,' you'll find a partner you haven't paired up with before and wait for further directions.")

4. Give directions one at a time. If there are numerous steps, post them at the front of the classroom.

5. Scan students' faces and body language for readiness. If students are ready, proceed with the activity. If they seem confused, repeat the directions in a different way. If they are not buying into the activity, go back to the first step and try a different hook.

6. Start the activity by giving the trigger word. ("Go!")

Rule #5: Show Your Passion

The final rule for engagement relates to nonverbal communication—possibly the most powerful communication form. Research (Wild, Erb, & Bartels, 2001) suggests that feelings are contagious. Our own facial muscles mimic the expressions of the faces we see in photographs, in movies, or at a sporting event, whether those faces are sad, happy, disgusted, or joyful (Dimberg & Thunberg, 1998). When students see you teach, they unconsciously feel your feelings. As teachers, you can positively affect students' states of mind simply by being in a positive state. If you enjoy your job, show your passion!

It's not enough to feel that teaching is your calling; you need to demonstrate passion so that your students can feel it, too. Passion is a very powerful classroom motivator (Brophy, 2004). Passion tells students that you care about what you do and that you're connecting with them. Passion gets students curious, excited, and even inspired. And passion cannot be faked. If you're not passionate in your teaching, your students will see right through you. They can sense when a teacher is just going through the motions.

That leaves you with one choice: be excited to come to work every day. Good teachers find ways to get more interested in what they are teaching and to make things more interesting for their students. It requires a little more work, a little more imagination, and maybe even a little acting ability:

passionate teachers get their message across not only with words but also with body language, or nonverbal messages. They exude raw energy: their bodies sway and their hands gesticulate animatedly, their voices fluctuate, and they physically orient themselves toward their students, intent on conveying their enthusiasm.

Feeling passionate about your work will ensure that your body language matches your verbal messages. This is crucial because students pick up nonverbal cues from their teachers' facial muscles quickly—usually in under 50 milliseconds (Carbon, 2011). Remember, feelings are contagious. Students respond well to positive body language, if not out of respect for their teacher's passion, then through the unconscious habit of mimicry.

Solutions You Can Use

Stay active. Move around your classroom; do not get stuck up front. Refer to posters on the wall, use props, and gesticulate dramatically. Be dynamic! Students will notice your expression and gestures and engage accordingly.

Vary your voice purposefully. If you tend to speak in a monotone, replace it with interesting and often unpredictable voice fluctuation. Vary your tone and add pauses—sometimes for drama and sometimes just to help students process the content. Let your voice demonstrate your enthusiasm.

Keep your eyes focused on students. Avoid looking at your computer, notes, desk, or any other nonstudent destination. Making eye contact shows that you care about and respect your students and that you're attending to them fully. Look into their eyes and be excited!

Be positive. Focus on what you want to happen rather than the negatives. Be in love with the content and your methods. Instead of saying, "I know you guys don't usually like doing this, but . . . ," sell the positives, believe in your message, and show your excitement. Make sure you are sincere, honest, and straight with students. They dislike sarcasm, and it often generates distrust over time. Finally, remember to nurture your own passion. Use music that gets you excited. Wear comfortable shoes, practice healthy habits, and use positive self-talk to stay relaxed and focused. Chapter 9 (pp. 167–169) goes further in depth on how to alleviate stress and find more joy in your own life.

Making the Magic Happen

Beginning teachers are often on a perpetual search for the next quick and easy strategy, but over time, taking that path burns them out and drains their optimism. If you're the same teacher you've always been, then nothing will change. Making micro-tweaks will not give you dramatically better results. However, when the five rules for engagement are in place and used consistently, classroom strategies simply work better. By understanding the rules, you'll see that the magic is within you, not an individual activity.

In the chapters that follow, you'll read some true stories of how teachers in high-poverty schools are getting over-the-top results. Everything you read about has already been done—and has worked. You'll learn more smart, purposeful, research-based strategies that will help you make the magic happen in your own classroom. Get ready for some challenges and solutions, beginning with classroom climate in Chapter 3.

3

Engage for Positive Climate

The Connecting Engagement Factors

- **Vocabulary:** In a positive climate, students feel safe enough to take risks and try out new words, resulting in stronger vocabulary retention.
- **Effort and energy:** In a positive climate, students feel affirmed and are motivated to work harder.
- **Mind-set:** A positive climate fosters a mind-set of academic optimism and confidence.
- **Cognitive capacity:** A mind-set of academic optimism makes students more receptive to learning and expanding their repertoire of cognitive skills.
- **Relationships:** In a positive, emotionally safe climate, relationships thrive.
- **Stress level:** In a positive climate, students are in more relaxed mind-body states and feel a sense of control over their own learning, resulting in less unhealthy stress and more healthy stress.

In the Classroom

Dan is a veteran 3rd grade teacher at a Title I school. Last school year, 66 percent of the students entering his class were scoring at or above grade level in reading. After a year in his class, only 48 percent scored at grade level, and none scored above it. In fact, his students performed worse than did most 3rd graders in other Title I schools who had similar incoming scores.

During an end-of-year interview about his teaching, Dan spent most of the time complaining. He said, "What with the testing and the responsibility and keeping up with the behavior reports and the data, it has gotten so much harder over the years. It's more work than it used to be, and we don't get the time to be creative." He admitted that he had tried engagement strategies, but they never seemed to catch on. He was quiet for a moment, then shrugged and said, "You just don't know the kids I have. They've got a lot going on at home."

Katherine, another 3rd grade teacher, is just down the hallway, but her classroom is a world away from Dan's. The engagement is over the top: students are moving around, participating in activities, and interacting with one another. Music is playing, and the students are smiling. It's obvious that they love being in Katherine's class. On top of everything, their reading scores are excellent.

During Katherine's end-of-year interview, she counted her blessings: "With all the challenges this year, I'm so glad the kids are helping out. It just makes my job so much easier. Yeah, teaching involves more work nowadays, but I love my job, and I really feel like these kids need me. I feel like I make a difference." She doesn't mention the students' backgrounds or complain about what they do wrong in class. When Katherine's students enter her classroom, they leave their problems at the door.

Comparing the classrooms of Dan and Katherine, we see two starkly different pictures emerge: kids dread being in Dan's class, and they love being in Katherine's class. But the difference doesn't lie in the kids. Kids have roller-coaster emotions and pretty much go the same direction the wind is blowing. Plus, students come and go every year.

Teachers are the common denominator, and the key factor affecting class climate. They are much more than weather reporters who simply observe or react to class climate; they are the creators of the class climate and, as such, have a huge influence on students' engagement, learning, and overall daily lives. If your class climate is not as positive as Katherine's, then it's time for an overhaul.

Five Actions to Create a Positive Class Climate

This chapter will help you begin the process of developing an "engagement climate." When you enter a classroom, the energy—whether positive or negative—is almost immediately apparent. Positive, high-energy classrooms reflect passionate, skillful, and smart teaching. Many factors combine to create a positive class climate, and make no mistake: a positive climate is not just about good relationships between teachers and students. Although relationships are an essential building block of a positive climate, they alone do not make the magic happen. Students may like and even respect a teacher while still sitting there like inert lumps of coal waiting for a spark.

A positive class climate is filled with what has been termed "academic optimism" (Hoy, Tarter, & Woolfolk-Hoy, 2006). When the class's physical and emotional energy is high and flush with hope and optimism, students try harder and enjoy the learning more. Teachers with a strong class climate model a passion for learning, and their students buy into it.

For most students living in poverty, a positive, engaging classroom is more a dream than a reality. A national study (Pianta et al., 2007) of 2,500 elementary classrooms across 400 school districts, all with highly qualified, credentialed teachers, found that *fewer than 10 percent of poor children experienced highly positive class climates*. The data indicate that the problem is not that poor students *can't* learn, but that 90 percent of teachers don't give them a *chance* to learn. This chapter lays out five actions you can take to create a positive climate and give every student a chance to learn in your classroom.

Five Actions to Create a Positive Class Climate

1. Raise the bar.
2. Manage mind-body states.
3. Establish that "we are family."
4. Sustain emotional positivity.
5. Teach positive social and emotional responses.

Action #1: Raise the Bar

The *normalcy bias* is a psychological principle we use to predict the future based on the past, regardless of how "non-normal" it might be. Our experiences, over time, gradually create our norms. Common behaviors and climates experienced over time gradually create expectations for what is normal. Some children grow up in Third World countries where there is no fresh water, no reliable source of food, marginal schools, and rampant disease. If this is their environment from birth, it feels normal. For many teachers, "normal" is a classroom where a few students raise their hands, a few sleep or act out, and the rest stay quiet. When the bell rings, the students shuffle out numbly into the daylight, perhaps hoping for a better experience elsewhere. Teachers with classes like these might say, "That's how the kids are. What would you *expect* to see?"

These teachers see both student behavior and their own teaching as fixed. That's an unfortunate mistake. For years, educators have been told to raise their expectations of students, and research supports raising the bar. Teachers' expectations are critical to student success. One study (Coe, 2002) found that teachers' expectations of students had a staggering 1.03 effect size on student achievement. Students typically live out their own expectations, so effective teachers get students to expect more of themselves. Students who have low expectations of themselves typically underperform. And remember to expect more of yourself, too. You should aim to be to such an effective, engaging teacher that students thank you at the end of class.

Jamie Irish, an award-winning 8th grade teacher at a low-income public secondary school in New Orleans, understands the importance of raising the bar. He challenges his students to outscore the far more affluent students at the neighboring Lusher Charter School (academically ranked number 4 in the state) on the district tests. His battle cry of "Crush Lusher" fosters a Super Bowl–level fever of mission, motivation, and teamwork. Students see class time as preparation to win the near-impossible victory and prove that they are just as good as their high-scoring rivals. Have you set the bar that high in your classroom?

Solutions You Can Use

Refer to the learning destination as a certainty. Whenever you give an assignment, rather than saying, "If you finish . . . ," say instead, "When you complete this . . . ." Assume your students will succeed, and always look forward: "Once we get here, we'll go for this next goal." Keep optimism high. Tell your class, "Stick with our plan. I'm on your side, and I won't let you fail." Expressing confidence in learning outcomes indicates your belief both in students and in yourself.

Don't have low-performing students set long-term achievement goals for themselves. What low-performing students perceive as their personal best may be quite different from their potential; many are happy just to pass a class. You need to be the one to set long-term goals (see the next solution). In the short term, you just want to see students make improvements every week. Have them set mini-goals, such as completing a 30-minute team assignment.

Start setting "superb" as the goal. To get students on the road to success, set long-term goals a mile high! Then provide the capacity and the attitudes to help students reach that goal. Once you have set high achievement goals for the class, help students believe in their ability to achieve the goals by demonstrating *how* they will succeed. One teacher I know tells students that their goal is to earn either an *A* or a *B* for the class; nothing less is acceptable. She then promises them, "Stick with me, and I'll help you reach your goal."

Affirm every little success early on. After checking to see how well students did on an assignment, affirm their success: "How many of you got 80 percent or more correct? YES! Turn to your neighbor and say, 'I did it!'" Once students develop a stronger belief in themselves, dial back the positive affirmations from "overwhelming" to "strong."

Action #2: Manage Mind-Body States

Struggling teachers often complain about students' personalities or character. Those complaints are based on a faulty understanding of developmental stages. Young kids usually have limited control over their own minute-by-minute micro-behaviors. They are simply not very good at regulating their own states for hours on end, especially in boring classrooms. To compensate, you'll need to manage their states more.

What do I mean by "states"? Students' thoughts, emotions, behaviors, and academic performance correlate with their physical, emotional, and cognitive states (Jensen, 2003). These mind-body states are affected by hundreds of moments each day. The broad state of "how we are doing" encompasses sensations (hunger, tiredness, itchiness); emotions (anger, sadness, joy); and attitudes and beliefs (optimistic, gullible, focused) (see Figure 3.1).

Figure 3.1 Sample Mind-Body States

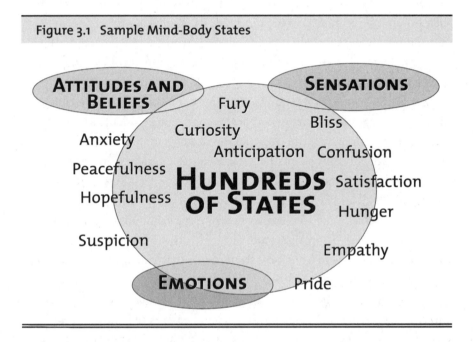

Students show up to class in a variety of states; usually, they are in their primary attractor states. An *attractor state* may be defined as the preferred or default state toward which conditions or systems tend to move. In other words, people become attracted to states according to their frequency of occurrence. As the brain strengthens repeated neural networks over time, these attractor states become habitual. Soon, these states become comfort zones.

For example, some students are angry a lot because anger is their primary attractor state, or "default" state. When bad things happen—which is often the case among low-SES students—stress levels increase, hope diminishes, and anger feels normal. When you see anger or apathy in your classroom, take a deep breath and exhale your stress slowly.

Other states that obstruct learning include frustration, hunger, skepticism, fear, or sleepiness. Apathy is sadly common. One study (Shernoff et al., 2003) found that one in six students were bored in every single class, and almost half experienced boredom and disengagement every day. Students reported that they were in a state of apathy for more than 25 percent of each day.

When your students appear to be angry or apathetic, avoid judging them or reacting out of exasperation or pity. Students don't choose their parents, their home environments, or their upbringing. Yelling at, criticizing, or demeaning students for misbehavior does not reap good behavior; on the contrary, it will drive students to hate school, disconnect from learning, and maybe even drop out.

Instead, let your understanding of students' mind-body states enable you to better manage class climate. Rather than punishing students for negative states or just hoping they show up in optimal states for learning, take charge and gently, purposefully shape their states yourself. Students in positive states have better mind-sets and stronger attention skills (Rowe, Hirsh, & Anderson, 2006) and demonstrate more appropriate behavior (Fredrickson & Branigan, 2005). Teachers have an extraordinary amount of influence during the relatively short time students are in class. Strong teachers take the actions necessary to transform students' negative incoming states into positive target states (see Figure 3.2).

The best way to start shaping student states is to build strong relationships. When we like and respect those around us, we are naturally in safer, more positive states. It is also important to provide some variety. Shift the social conditions in your class frequently, moving smoothly from whole-class instruction to partner work to individual work to small-group work. Be sure to add energizers every 10 to 20 minutes, and notice how quick movement, social contact, and verbal requests tend to keep students in positive states for learning. In addition to the strategies I list in the following section, use any of the buy-in strategies from Chapter 2 or the energizers provided in Chapter 7.

Many teachers lament that they never have enough time to teach the required curriculum content. But think about it: during a big chunk of their day, students are in poor states for learning. Teachers spend about 20

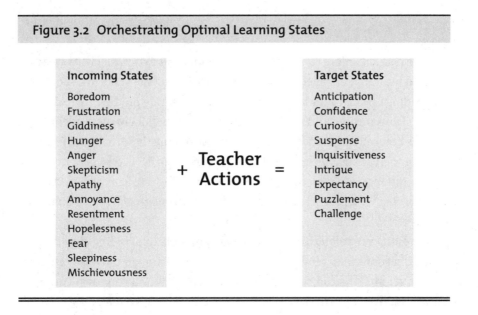

Figure 3.2 Orchestrating Optimal Learning States

Incoming States

Boredom
Frustration
Giddiness
Hunger
Anger
Skepticism
Apathy
Annoyance
Resentment
Hopelessness
Fear
Sleepiness
Mischievousness

+ **Teacher Actions** =

Target States

Anticipation
Confidence
Curiosity
Suspense
Inquisitiveness
Intrigue
Expectancy
Puzzlement
Challenge

percent of the school day on classroom and time management (Pianta et al., 2007). Savvy teachers who cultivate positive student states can end up getting back that precious 20 percent to make a real difference in student achievement.

Solutions You Can Use

Reduce lecture time. Instead of delivering long lectures, limit your talk time to short chunks: 5 to 8 minutes for elementary classes and 8 to 12 minutes for secondary classes. Then, allow students to begin processing the content for greater understanding—for example, by writing a summary, creating a quiz, or teaching a partner. Students will be less bored or overwhelmed and in a better state for learning.

Eliminate the "fight, flight, or freeze" response. Avoid triggering students' acute stress responses by keeping the classroom atmosphere emotionally safe. For each reprimand you deliver, offer at least three positive affirmations. If you must reprimand a student, do it in private. Never embarrass students in front of their peers, and never use sarcasm or put-downs. A student whom you put down in front of his or her peers will likely hold a grudge or want to get even. If you make that mistake, apologize to the student after class.

Give students more control. Letting students make some decisions leads them to feel more engaged because they have a personal stake in the class's proceedings. When they're coming up with and acting on their own ideas, they feel empowered and excited to follow through. Encourage students to have a more vested interest in class by broadening their roles and giving them more responsibilities. Involve them in making decisions, generating quiz questions, resolving discipline issues, choosing music to play in class, and working with partners to come up with class energizers (more on this in Chapter 7).

Ask more compelling questions. Engage students by avoiding closed-ended questions like "How many branches of government did our Founding Fathers set up?" Instead, ask, "If you were going to found your own country, how would you govern it? Why would you choose that system?"

Keep students in suspense. Foster students' sense of curiosity. For example, introduce a math problem by saying, "How would you like to know how to solve this math problem in half the time it used to take you? I'll show you how in just a moment." Or keep students guessing with a follow-the-directions energizer: "If you'd like to wake up your brain, please stand up. Now, touch the backs of nine chairs. Good. Next, find a partner and then raise your hand. Once you know his or her name, shout it out. Perfect. Now, tell your partner something you are looking forward to in the next two weeks."

Action #3: Establish That "We Are Family"

In 1979, the Pittsburgh Pirates won the World Series, beating the Baltimore Orioles in a dramatic seven-game series. The team's theme song was Sister Sledge's huge pop hit "We Are Family." The winning players credited their team's "family atmosphere" for their strong performance. Is your class a close-knit family? Or is it "every student for himself"?

A classroom's social glue is not just an extra enhancement; it has real academic significance. With a strong 0.72 effect size, student-teacher relationships are in the top 10 of all student achievement factors, and group cohesion and peer influences have a strong 0.53 effect size (Hattie, 2008).

Contrast these with the surprisingly low 0.09 effect size for teacher content knowledge (Hattie, 2008).

Every classroom includes multiple layers of relationships that matter. These different types of relationships include teacher-to-student (does the teacher care about and respect each student?); teacher-to-class (does the teacher treat the class as a close family?); student-to-teacher (does each student respect and like the teacher?); student-to-student (does each student feel included?); and staff-to-staff (do students see adults working together in a healthy manner?). Each of these relationships has its own purpose and effect, and each can be positively influenced by the teacher.

Often, low-SES students have no stable adult role models, so teachers need to embrace the "parent" (matriarch or patriarch) role in school. Treating your class as a family can reduce discipline issues and improve learning. For example, social bonding and trust help mitigate the adverse effects of chronic stress by prompting the brain to release oxytocin, a neuropeptide that suppresses the "classic" stress hormones, such as cortisol (Kosfeld, Heinrichs, Zak, Fischbacher, & Fehr, 2005; Leuner, Caponiti, & Gould, 2012).

From a developmental perspective, by about age 7 or 8, children become more interested in affiliation among peers (e.g., having friends come to a birthday party). By the time they reach age 12 or 13, children focus on social status and want to feel special among peers. A loss of social status among peers can increase stress level (Kozorovitskiy & Gould, 2004) and cause real physical pain (Eisenberger, Jarcho, Lieberman, & Naliboff, 2006). Middle school students without friends show lower levels of prosocial behavior, lower academic achievement, and greater emotional distress than do students who have reciprocal friendships (Wentzel, Barry, & Caldwell, 2004). The social areas of the brain actually overlap with most of the cognitive areas (Adolphs, 2003), and the relationship among cooperative learning, social support, and academic achievement is strong (Ghaith, 2002). Cooperative learning has a significant positive influence on student achievement, with an effect size of 0.72 (Hattie, 2008). Yet many uninformed teachers spend class time keeping students from interacting.

This is shortsighted and unwise. In today's world of all-pervasive social networking, online gaming, and file sharing, it is incomprehensible that a classroom teacher would have students work in isolation all day. Regardless of whether you teach at the prekindergarten, elementary, or secondary level, you should invest at least half of your class time in some kind of social interaction. The stakes are high. If you don't let students find peer affiliation through cooperative groups, clubs, or teams, they'll find it in cliques or even gangs. If you don't build students' status in class by giving affirmations, letting students show their uniqueness, and encouraging peer approval, they'll seek status outside school through risky behaviors or criminal activities. If you provide what students need in a healthy way, odds are they won't seek it out in unhealthy ways.

When all members of the class are working together toward a positive learning effort, they build a collective social power. Such a class provides a safe, welcoming place for students to take risks, make errors, learn from one another, provide feedback, discuss goals and criteria for success, and build positive relationships with one another and the teacher. Humans are hardwired to be social (Castiello et al., 2010), so let's not fight against our instincts. The data are clear: better relationships support better achievement.

Solutions You Can Use

The model of "class as family" has gained credence as a strong academic booster. This section provides solutions to help strengthen two types of classroom relationships: teacher-to-student and student-to-student.

Adopt the "parent" role in your class. To build positive relationships with your students, try to discover one new thing (e.g., an achievement or a family milestone) about at least one student in each class, every day. Learn every student's strengths or unique talents, then build on those strengths tactfully, and encourage students to display their talents in front of their peers. Acknowledge all students' contributions in class, and hold weekly wholeclass talks, family meeting–style. Make sure to smile at all your students— not just your favorites—and always use personal courtesies like "please," "thank you," and "pardon me."

Form cooperative groups (elementary). At the elementary level, place students in cooperative groups of four, making sure the composition of each group is heterogeneous in terms of student achievement level. Allow students to pick which team member gets to play each key role: leader, recorder, starter, encourager, and so on. Ensure that you set up these groups to succeed. Visit www.behavioradvisor.com/CoopLearning.html for helpful tips on implementing cooperative learning in your classroom.

Start replacing certain teacher-centered activities with cooperative-learning activities. For example, instead of reading aloud to students, have cooperative groups engage in a read-around activity, where each group member gets a turn to read. Allow time for students to pause if they need it. Ask students to discuss an issue question or to review or critique the reading with their groups. Encourage students to fully collaborate as a group in which each member has something of value to contribute to its collective effort.

Form cooperative teams (secondary). At the secondary level, place students in teams of five, grouping them by interest, not achievement level. Let each team pick its own name, leader, and cheer, as well as half of its goals (you select the other, core half of the goals). Have the teams work together on projects, brainstorming, and problem solving. For example, in a social studies class, teams could work on projects such as coming up with a recycling plan for their community. Switch up the teams every four to six weeks.

Create the "class glue" with get-to-know-you activities. Build trust and camaraderie by having students write down responses to at least one prompt or question each week and share their answers with their group or team members. Possible prompts include

- Name an object that is important to you.
- Name a life value that is important to you.
- Describe something good that has happened to you recently.
- Name a dream of something you want in your life when you're 25 years old.
- Share something most people don't know about you that they should know.

Do your students know every other kid in their class by name? Occasionally, have students form pairs outside their cooperative groups or teams and take some time to get to know each other, with each student completing the following sentences about his or her new partner:

1. One thing my neighbor likes to do is _____.
2. My neighbor owns a _____.
3. Someday, my neighbor would like to _____.
4. My neighbor is good at _____.
5. My neighbor gets excited about _____.

Help students gain social status. One way to help neutralize the adverse effects of social status disparity is to follow a school uniform policy. Even if your school doesn't have one, there are still steps you can take. One Title I school that had problems with dress code compliance addressed the issue simply by requiring every student to wear black pants every day, except the last Friday of each month, when students could wear whatever they wanted. This solved the "bottom half" of the issue quickly, because no uniforms were necessary.

Also make sure to provide opportunities for students to gain positive social status. For example, invite them to read a powerful composition they've written in front of their peers. Come up with and distribute awards to students for exemplifying qualities like creativity, enthusiasm, and leadership. A whole class can gain status by winning a schoolwide competition or by putting on a school event. The goal is not so much for all students to feel "equal" as it is for each student to feel special in a different way.

Action #4: Sustain Emotional Positivity

James Brown's 1965 hit "I Got You (I Feel Good)" is one of the most popular, widely played songs of all time. It is on the soundtrack of countless movies and TV shows and can be heard at sporting events and concerts worldwide. Perhaps part of the reason the song is still so resonant today is simply that people like to feel good. Which brings me to an important question: do students feel good in your class? I'm serious. When students don't feel connected or affirmed, why should they bother coming to school?

Emotions have become a hot research topic during the last 10 years. Here's what we now know: scientists no longer consider emotions to be a "frill." Emotional positivity is essential to learning and productivity. Upbeat states boost overall happiness (Fredrickson & Joiner, 2002) and psychological growth for learning (Fredrickson, Tugade, Waugh, & Larkin, 2003), both of which are fundamental to cognitive and behavioral growth. Positivity also lowers levels of cortisol (Steptoe, Wardle, & Marmot, 2005), thus reducing the effects of chronic stress and such symptoms as impulsivity and poor short-term memory. As a bonus, positive emotions help reduce absences and boost resilience to adversity (Fredrickson et al., 2003; van Wouwe, Band, & Ridderinkhof, 2011).

In a fascinating study, researchers (Hart & Risley, 1995) placed recording devices, with adult consent, in 42 homes and recorded hundreds of hours of everyday conversations over the course of two years. The researchers then analyzed the conversations and categorized each one as affirming (positive), reprimanding (negative), or neutral. Among higher-income families, the ratio of positive conversations to negative conversations was 6 to 1. The numbers shifted dramatically for middle-income families, with a 2-to-1 positive-to-negative ratio. In lower-income families, the ratio shifted even further in the same direction, with a 1-to-2 positive-to-negative ratio. Since this study, research (Catalino & Fredrickson, 2011) has found that the optimal ratio of positives to negatives for human growth is 3 to 1.

Teachers often tell me their students are angry and grumpy. If you grew up hearing only one affirmation for every two reprimands, you'd be grumpy, too! The last thing low-SES students need is a critical, hostile school experience. If a student's only one-on-one interaction with the teacher is a reprimand for a discipline infraction, that's all the student will remember that day. If it happens often enough, the student will internalize a deep dislike of the teacher and of school in general. So avoid sending students home with continued daily "deficits." No one can afford to have bad days like that too often. If you want your students to be in a good state for learning, make sure you offer three positive affirmations for every one reprimand or error correction. Not all of the positives need to come from the teacher; they can come from peers, too. Your classroom should provide an upbeat and affirming experience for every student, every day—no exceptions. On any random day, if a visitor sat in your class, what ratio of positives to negatives would they find? The following strategies will help ensure that your classroom is a safe and thriving community.

Solutions You Can Use

Use emotional punctuation. When students do well, whether individually or within a team, ensure they get kudos for their achievement. A positive affirmation may include a smile or gesture, an oral or written affirmation, or a positive peer comment. You might open class with a group affirmation like, "If you made it to class on time, raise your hand and say 'Yes!'"

Pump up positive classroom responses. When students participate in class, affirm their effort (and the risk they took) by saying, "Thank you for jumping in!" Or affirm the content of a student's answer with something like "I hadn't thought of that—that's creative!"

Experiment with saying "yes" to students' requests as often as possible. If they suggest, "How about no homework this weekend?" reply, "Sure—as long as we accomplish [XYZ] before class is over." If a student asks, "Can I take a bathroom break?" say, "Yes, as soon as we finish this."

Accentuate the positive. Make sure your class acknowledges its own success through peer affirmations ("Turn to your neighbor and say, 'You're moving up fast!'"); team celebrations of project completions (each class team can have its own); and affirming class music (e.g., play a song like "Always Look on the Bright Side" by Costa Crew).

Never make threats; frame admonishments positively. Instead of saying, "If you do that one more time . . . !" say, "Here's how you can stay out of trouble today: remain seated and save the extra talking until our break in a few minutes. Will you do that, please?"

Use variety in your clapping celebrations. For a sense of novelty and fun, switch up your applause methods. For example, give applause by moving your clapping hands in the shape of a circle for a "round" of applause. Or have students give a triple snap of the fingers, then let out a big "Hooray!" while throwing their arms up.

Raise students' expectations about their potential to go to college. Start mentally programming low-SES students to believe that when it comes to their own potential, the sky is the limit. Instill in them the expectation that they, just like their affluent peers, can attend college. If no one does this for students, why would we expect them to have postgraduation aspirations? I cofounded an academic enrichment program that holds events on college campuses. After spending a week at the beautiful Stanford University campus, for example, students who have always thought that "college is not for me" quickly upgrade their aspirations! The Adopt-A-College Program (www.adopt-a-college.org) sets a similarly inspirational example. Each year, elementary and middle school classrooms in the program "adopt" a college, wear college T-shirts, write to college pen pals, and are promised scholarships. The program has dramatically decreased dropout rates and increased college attendance among participating students.

Action #5: Teach Positive Social and Emotional Responses

Every day in schools around the world, teachers get frustrated with students' distracting behavior. The teachers ask or tell the students to behave better. The students respond with a smirk or a wisecrack or by blowing bubbles with their gum. The teachers say, "Don't give me that attitude!" No one is happy, and things go downhill from there.

What is going on in this scenario? And why do students growing up in adversity in particular have so many discipline issues? One possibility is that the *teacher* has the attitude, not the student. At birth, our brains are hardwired with just six emotions: joy, anger, sadness, surprise, fear, and disgust (Ekman, 2004). Any additional emotional responses must be learned (Sauter, Eisner, Ekman, & Scott, 2010), which is less likely to happen in low-SES households. Children growing up in poverty or other adverse circumstances get less quality time with their caregivers (Fields & Casper, 2001) and thus hear fewer affirming words. Their caregivers are less likely to provide security, warmth, and sensitivity, which means kids are more likely to be anxious or withdrawn (Evans, 2004).

Ideal classroom emotions include cooperativeness, patience, humility, and gratitude. Students who don't have those in their emotional repertoires can show only what they *do* have. The student who smirked may be showing disgust, which is what he is feeling. He doesn't know the desired response (likely penitence or humility), and he believes that he is being chastised for something that is not his fault. It's very frustrating for both parties, but it is not helpful to blame the students.

Low-SES students act out as a result of many of the same things that irk their more affluent peers: irrelevant content, rude teachers, or lack of academic assets (such as reading fluency, study skills, memory skills, or background knowledge). The difference is that they are just more likely to have difficulty displaying the appropriate emotions (Schultz, Izard, Ackerman, & Youngstrom, 2001).

Students who do not show appropriate social-emotional responses in class need an adult to give them the tools to survive and thrive in the world outside their neighborhoods. Make it your mission to teach students appropriate responses, for their sake as well as your own. These are teachable skills, and the research (Izard et al., 2001) suggests that they are a huge predictor of future social and academic outcomes—even as early as kindergarten (Trentacosta & Izard, 2007).

Solutions You Can Use

Model appropriate responses. At the elementary level, demonstrate positive social-emotional responses to the entire class and let students mimic you. Talk about the contexts in which the new responses are appropriate.

At the secondary level, ask a student who fails to display the context-appropriate emotion or seems to have an "attitude" to stay for a moment after class. Sit down with the student and say, "Listen, you're a good kid. Earlier, I was expecting you to show [appropriate emotion], and you didn't. Most adults will expect *this* [show the desired response]. I know that's not what you would normally do, but adults expect it, and I want you to stay out of trouble. Let me show you what I was looking and listening for." Using this one-on-one time to strengthen your relationship rather than to punish the student will get you on the road toward success.

Teach responses with fun activities. For example, set up simple student role-plays (or game-like formats, such as charades) in which students take turns showing an emotion while their partners or team members try to match it or label it. Then the team can discuss when that emotion is appropriate. You could also show video clips depicting various behaviors of kids the same age as your students, and lead a whole-class discussion to identify and analyze the behaviors.

The Greatest Gift

It's not students' job to change their lives to make their school work better. It is up to schools to adapt to work better for students. One of the most important factors affecting student engagement and achievement is class climate, and it's under your control. Remember: you are more than the weather reporter; you are the weather *creator!*

Lasting positive climates are not predicated on having "good" students; they are thoughtfully planned and consistently orchestrated by caring, savvy professionals. Help students forget about anything else in the world except the positive energy and caring relationships inside your classroom. I know that your classroom climate won't transform overnight. But if you take what's in this chapter seriously, you can do it. A positive climate is one of the greatest gifts a teacher can give his or her students, and in a way, this opportunity we have to change students' lives is a gift for us, too.

4

Engage to Build Cognitive Capacity

The Connecting Engagement Factors

- **Vocabulary:** Many activities can use vocabulary to train students' working memory, and increased working memory in turn helps students retain vocabulary.
- **Mind-set:** Communicating to students that their cognitive capacity is not fixed empowers them and creates a growth mind-set that enables them to dream of doing even better.
- **Cognitive capacity:** Teaching and reinforcing core cognitive skills lays the groundwork for further learning and boosts students' ability to reason and solve problems in unfamiliar contexts, across the curriculum and over the long term.
- **Stress level:** Learning skills like self-control and goal setting clarifies behavioral expectations and classroom processes and shows students that they have control over their actions and certain outcomes, which reduces stress and creates a sense of self-efficacy.

In the Classroom

Colleen ranted, "These kids have no clue. They don't remember what I said. Day after day, no one is paying attention. Even *if* they pay attention, they don't follow directions. And even *if* they follow directions, they don't work on the problems. They just sit there. Sometimes I hate my job."

Colleen's colleague Josh could feel the frustration. He paused a moment and then offered an observation: "I think there's a disconnect here that's common in our field. As educators, we're told, 'Be clear: tell kids exactly what you want.' It *seems* to make sense. After all, shouldn't we be clear on what we're telling kids to do?"

"Yes, of course. So what's the problem?" Colleen replied.

Josh continued: "You assume that if you tell kids exactly *what* to do, then they should do it. But paying focused attention is a learned skill, and so is holding ideas in your head. Prioritizing and processing information are also learned skills. Maybe your students just don't know *how* to do those things. If you're not teaching them, it's probably not going to happen."

Colleen fell silent. It had never occurred to her that students might not know how to do the tasks she asked of them. She just assumed they had an attitude problem. Suddenly, her long-held conception of how to teach was upended. "Oh," she murmured. "I just never thought of that. So . . . how do I teach those skills?"

Five Actions to Build Cognitive Capacity

Recent research (Sheridan, Sarsour, Jutte, D'Esposito, & Boyce, 2012) demonstrates an association between parental socioeconomic status and children's executive function skills—the crucial thinking processes that manage other thinking processes, including problem solving, critical thinking, processing speed, attention, self-control, and working memory. Although some children have already begun attaining these skills by the time they start school, children who grow up poor are less likely to have this necessary academic foundation.

The good news is that high-quality classroom instruction can build students' core cognitive capacities. Cognition and intelligence, as determined by such measures as IQ, are not fixed but malleable (Buschkuehl & Jaeggi, 2010) and can be profoundly affected by positive, enriching experiences. In one adoption study, researchers (Duyme, Dumaret, & Tomkiewicz, 1999) identified 65 low-SES children who were adopted between the ages of 4 and 6 and had a mean IQ of 77 (the median is 100). After eight years of sustained positive experiences, the children were retested in early adolescence. This time, their mean IQ score was 91—an average gain of 14 IQ points. Certain adopted children who were given additional enhanced conditions for the eight years boosted their IQs by nearly 20 points! Schools have kids for *13 years*. Think about the difference we can make in that amount of time.

One of the best things teachers can do is foster *fluid intelligence*, or students' ability to use learned skills and thought processes to reason and solve problems in new, unfamiliar contexts. Fluid intelligence is a highly transferable skill that will serve your students well in the real world—and it can be taught. One study (Jaeggi, Buschkuehl, Jonides, & Perrig, 2008) found that 19 days of training on working memory strengthened both memory and fluid intelligence. The more hours of training students receive, the greater the effects.

Teaching thinking skills is one of the most effective ways to boost academic success. In terms of student achievement, teaching cognitive skills has a significant 0.69 effect size, and teaching study skills has a similarly strong 0.59 effect size (Hattie, 2011). This chapter lays out five actions you can take to build students' cognitive capacity.

Five Actions to Build Cognitive Capacity

1. Build attention skills.
2. Teach problem solving and critical thinking.
3. Train working memory.
4. Develop processing speed.
5. Foster self-control.

The engagement strategies in this chapter will help you build your students' thinking and learning skills, but keep in mind that fully developing these skills requires more than the occasional fun activity. If you want to see remarkable results, I recommend focusing on these skills for at least 10 minutes a day for 6 to 10 weeks. You can easily embed this chapter's strategies into your existing curriculum, so you don't need to take extra time to teach these skills.

Action #1: Build Attention Skills

Have you ever ordered your class, "Pay attention!"? When students pay attention, academic achievement usually goes up (Silverman, Davids, & Andrews, 1963). Yet the phrase "pay attention" is misleading. There are two primary types of attention, and the differences between them are important (see Figure 4.1).

Figure 4.1 Two Types of Attention

Hardwired and Reflexive	Learned and Earned
The student's brain automatically orients to safety, novelty, affiliation, contrast, movement, and risk/reward situations. In other words, quiet seatwork loses out to the DNA's priorities.	This complex skill set requires the student's brain to (1) disengage from the prior object of focus and (2) engage in and focus on a new object while (3) suppressing outside stimuli and (4) sustaining focus. This type of attention requires long practice.

The first type of attention is the hardwired variety: by nature, we are designed to orient our attention toward moving objects, rapid environmental changes, contrast, or novelty. The second type of attention—the one teachers ask for—refers to the learned skill of orienting attention in the desired direction, then sustaining that focus for as long as necessary while suppressing irrelevant distractions. It would be great if students would remain locked on what their teacher is trying to teach them, but it takes practice to suppress distracting outside stimuli and continually keep one's attention oriented toward the appropriate content or task. It takes readers, writers, chess players, musicians, and artists years to do it well.

Early attention skills are predictive of students' school success in the longer term, and unfortunately, students who were raised in poverty typically have weaker attention spans (Belsky, Pasco Fearon, & Bell, 2007; Rothbart & Bates, 2006). Fortunately, sustaining focused attention is a skill that can be taught. In the sections that follow, I offer both short-term workaround solutions and long-term skill-building strategies.

Short-Term Solutions You Can Use

Increase buy-in. Creating a hook that pulls students in to the task or content creates a genuine reason for students to pay attention. Use any of the buy-in strategies from Chapter 2, and consider giving small hints and teasers that prime students' interest in the upcoming content and make them more likely to attend to the lesson. Then add goal acquisition to the activity by getting students vested in reaching the target goal. For example, you might issue a challenge: "The last class was able to find only five differences. I bet you can do way better than that."

Use prediction. Ask students to make predictions about the upcoming lesson (e.g., about the content covered or process involved). Then get students vested in their predictions by making them public ("Raise your hand if you believe that . . ."). You can increase the stakes of the prediction by offering an incentive ("Those who make a correct prediction will get one free homework pass this month"). Prediction forces the brain to care about the outcome because we get vested in being right. Think about it: the Super Bowl is the most watched football game of the year not necessarily because it's the *best* game but because it's the most *bet-on* game. Prediction is powerful!

Pause and chunk. Every few minutes, pause for seven to nine seconds. These pauses both give students time to mentally process the content and add a sense of anticipation and importance to the lesson. Taking slightly longer breaks of 30 to 90 seconds may also help students focus (Ariga & Lleras, 2011). Dividing content into small "chunks" also supports attention and understanding. Keep your lectures short—5 to 8 minutes at the elementary level and 8 to 12 minutes at the secondary level. Then have students process the information through strategies like summarization, think-pair-share, or compare and contrast.

Engage in a fast physical activity. Break up the lesson with a quick-moving physical activity like Simon Says. This will boost the brain's levels of norepinephrine, a neurotransmitter that increases focus and attention. Chapter 7 provides many more examples of such physical activities.

Play Red Light, Purple Light. This activity builds attention and self-control in elementary-level students. In the traditional "Red Light, Green Light," a teacher acts as a traffic light by calling out "Red," "Green," or "Yellow," and students must start walking, then stop, go, or slow down accordingly. After students have mastered the original activity, switch it up by using different colors and even holding up different shapes to represent the actions (e.g., a purple square for "Go"). You can also use drumbeats to represent different actions: students walk quickly to fast drumming, slowly to slow drumming, and freeze when the drumming stops. Then turn it around and have students walk slowly to fast drum beats and quickly to slow drum beats.

Use "redirects." Novelty always generates attention. Ask students to redirect their attention to something unusual or quirky in the content or to another student who will help initiate a group activity. For example, if you say, "Quick, find a partner—you have nine seconds!" students will stop talking and immediately go into "search mode" to find a partner. You can also redirect students' attention through the use of a classroom ritual: say to the class, "Raise your hand if you'd like to do something we've never done before. Good. Now turn to your neighbor and say, 'I'm ready!'"

Long-Term Solutions You Can Use

Get students moving. Research shows a strong positive correlation between aerobic fitness and cognitive skills (Aberg et al., 2009; Hillman, Buck, Themanson, Pontifex, & Castelli, 2009; Niederer et al., 2011). In fact, physical exercise can increase the production of new brain cells (Pereira et al., 2007), which is highly correlated with learning, mood, and memory. For that reason, make sure your students get at least 20 minutes of exercise daily through physical education or recess, and never withhold recess from students as punishment for misbehavior. In the classroom, have students engage their sensory motor skills in such activities as crawling, climbing, or playing Simon Says or other games listed in Chapter 7. If possible, hone students' motor skills with agility challenges, such as going through an obstacle course or maintaining balance on a balance beam. All of these hone students' fine and gross motor skills and can strengthen focus and attention.

Provide practice. Whichever subject or grade level you teach, you can engage students in detailed, continual practice. Sustained practice strengthens students' ability to pay attention and suppress irrelevant stimuli, whether they are creating artwork, playing a sport, learning a musical instrument, working on a science project, or memorizing lines for the school play.

Teach students study skills. Help students learn to self-manage through such strategies as splitting goals into smaller tasks. Show them how to prioritize tasks by dividing them into categories labeled "urgent," "important," and "lower-priority." Teach and reinforce study skills like note taking, summarization, and pre-reading.

Use high-interest reading material. High-interest texts will do more than engage students; they will *compel* students to pay attention. If a student is passionate about cars, for example, then a book or article about cars is a great way to hook that student into reading. You might also have students read a brief article or story that ends in a cliffhanger, to be resolved when the reading continues another day. Leave them wanting more!

Conduct quick writes. Engaging students in quick, timed writing exercises develops their ability to focus. During quick writes, students write as fast as they can think, without having the luxury (or inhibition) of self-editing. This process builds students' capacity to stick with a topic over time. If you assign quick writes two to three times a week, over time, students will get better at focusing on one task at a time.

Action #2: Teach Problem Solving and Critical Thinking

Teaching problem solving and critical thinking builds students' cognitive capacity and has a strong influence on student achievement, with a 0.61 effect size (Hattie, 2008). Students with strong problem-solving skills are able to identify the real problem in a question posed and then prioritize and select steps for a path to a solution. Students with critical thinking skills are able to look at a problem from multiple perspectives, design a potential intervention, and then evaluate the outcome. Yet despite the incredible value of these skills, many teachers avoid explicit instruction in problem solving. Most simply don't realize that it can be taught, and those who do realize it don't know how.

Most kids who grow up in poverty don't have experience solving the kinds of academic problems offered up in class, and this process of teaching the brain to think critically and analytically requires support and practice. Initially, students' problem solving may seem slow, but by using the following solutions and providing opportunities to practice at least two or three times a week, you can help students become proficient problem solvers.

Solutions You Can Use

Model and scaffold the process. To teach a problem-solving model, begin by introducing a relevant problem that will get student buy-in—for example, for high schoolers, the problem might be, "How can I buy a car by the time I'm 18?" Then use a simple five-step process:

1. Walk the class through the steps of solving the problem.
2. Explain just how you did it.
3. Post the process that you just modeled and explained.
4. Give students a new problem and provide time for guided practice in using the new model and correcting errors.
5. Give students independent practice to continue internalizing the process.

Promote collaborative problem solving. Place students in pairs or small teams and then give the class a problem and a deadline to come up with the solution. The problem can be any type—a real-world dilemma or a mathematical word problem. Each pair or team must document the steps it takes in solving the problem and then report its answer. Next, give the class a different type of problem, like a relationship or family problem, and tell them to repeat the first problem-solving process they used to solve this new problem. In this way, students come up with their own models that work for solving different types of problems.

Teach transferable models for problem solving. To help students learn a new problem-solving model, give them the steps out of order. Working in pairs or small teams, the students have six minutes to put them in the correct order. Once they do that, they must come up with an example of a problem they solved using the model. Here are 10 steps of a sample problem-solving model (in correct sequence!):

1. Maintain a positive attitude. ("We can do this!")
2. Identify the real problem, watching out for extraneous details that take you off track.
3. State the goal.

4. Identify resources needed to solve the problem, including people, time, or tools.

5. Review boundaries or limitations of the problem-solving process, such as laws, policies, or time limits.

6. Identify potential paths to the solution—for example, the fastest, the cheapest, the most inclusive, and the safest paths.

7. Predict the risks or potential setbacks of each path.

8. Choose a strategy and write it out clearly.

9. Implement the strategy and tweak it as needed.

10. Celebrate success!

Create competition. Give the class a problem to solve and have students work in small teams, each one using a different problem-solving strategy. Assign or have teams choose strategies *before* they see the problem. For example, for a basic Algebra I math problem, a team could choose to draw a diagram, solve a similar but simpler problem first, work through the problem backward, use a formula it already knows, use logical reasoning, find a pattern and infer the solution, make a table or graph, or start with a guess and then check its work.

Action #3: Train Working Memory

Ever notice that some kids just can't seem to follow directions? Do the numbers drop out of their heads when they try to solve a math problem? Or do they forget what they're reading as soon as they've read it?

These are common symptoms of poor working memory. A strong working memory is critical to academic success. Peer-reviewed studies demonstrate that working memory predicts student performance in attentional tasks (Fukuda & Vogel, 2009), reading comprehension (Daneman & Carpenter, 1980), and reasoning and problem solving (Barrouillet & Lecas, 1999). Working memory also predicts performance in mathematics (De Smedt et al., 2009). In fact, working memory at age 5 *is a greater predictor of academic success* than IQ is at age 10 (Alloway & Alloway, 2010).

Unfortunately, low-SES students tend to have poorer working memories than their higher-SES peers do (Hackman & Farah, 2009). There are short-term, temporary workarounds teachers can use to support students with poor working memory, such as teaching in fewer, smaller chunks of content. Research (Gobet & Clarkson, 2004) suggests that an untrained working memory maxes out at one to two items, so chunking content makes sense. However, this strategy doesn't lead to long-term improvement in working memory (Elliott, Gathercole, Alloway, Holmes, & Kirkwood, 2010).

The best way to strengthen working memory is to train it. Fortu-nately, although it requires consistent practice, this is actually not difficult. Research (Salminen, Strobach, & Schubert, 2012) shows that building a strong working memory takes only 5 to 10 minutes of practice a day for 8 to 12 weeks. The great thing is that you can use existing content to teach it, so while you're building attentional skills and working memory, you're also reinforcing learning of the content. Working memory can even be success-fully taught to children with AD/HD (Holmes et al., 2010; Klingberg et al., 2005).

Working-memory content is stored in the brain as either sounds (e.g., a fire truck siren, a person's voice, a favorite song, or a dog barking) or images (pictures, movie scenes, social media, or scenery) (see Figure 4.2, p. 62). Life is full of combinations of both types of content: you can see and hear a person simultaneously as she speaks to you. But our brain tends to focus on one modality more than another at any given time. Accordingly, there is normally very little transfer from working-memory training in one modality type (sounds) to another (images).

To build working memory, start simple and *gradually* increase difficulty— over the course of weeks, not days. The more complex the working-memory training—the more you combine modalities by mixing visuals with sounds— the more likely it is that students will be able to generalize and transfer the skill being trained to various other tasks requiring executive functions (Thorell, Lindqvist, Bergman Nutley, Bohlin, & Klingberg, 2009). Keep in mind that skill transfer seems to be limited to the domain where it is used.

The following section provides strategies that address both domains. In addition to these, consider trying the activities on websites like www.junglememory.com (for younger students) and www.lumosity.com (for older students) to build students' attention skills and working memory. Both sites use brain-training software that is modeled on proven research.

Figure 4.2 How Working-Memory Content Is Stored

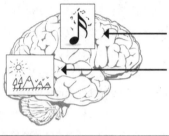

Working-memory content is always stored in the brain as either sounds (called a *phonological loop*) or images (or visual-spatial "sketchpad").

Solutions You Can Use

Note: some activities work better with younger students, and others with older students. But the bottom line is, there is no perfect activity; you'll likely need to experiment and adapt activities to work for your own students.

Practice recall. For five minutes a day, boost students' listening skills and working memory with simple, active games that require students to recall commands. Simon Says works very well for this purpose. You might say to the class, "Simon says, follow only the most recent command. Simon says, stand up *and* Simon says, put your hands on your head." Then change it up a bit: "Simon says, follow the first command and ignore the second. Simon says, clap twice and point to the exit sign."

Another recall activity to use is a clapping game. The beauty of this activity is its simplicity. Start with a very simple clap in front of the class—"Clap – clap"—that students must repeat. Then repeat the clap—"Clap – clap"— and, once again, have students repeat it. Next, start a new clapping pattern— "Clap – clap [pause] clap – clap"—for students to repeat. Pay attention to the sequence: it is important to start easy, then build up the complexity slowly, doubling back now and then to make sure students are keeping up. You should increase the complexity over the course of several weeks, doing the activity a few minutes a day, three to five times a week. Do not rush the process, and ensure everyone can keep up before moving to the next level. If you want to increase engagement, let a student lead the activity occasionally as a privilege or reward.

Use word baskets, file folders, and number bags. Elementary-level teachers can use the word basket activity (note: secondary-level teachers can use the same activity, just replacing the term "word basket" with "file folder") for five minutes a day in any content area as a pre-test for prior knowledge or as a review to reinforce content and build students' attentional skills and working memory. Group students into circles of four to six, then tell the class the name of the "basket"—that is, the content category within which students generate words. For example, if students are studying geography, you might say the word basket is "countries." The first student says, "Chile." The next student repeats, "Chile," and adds a new country, "France." The process continues with each student in the circle taking turns repeating the previous words *and* generating a new word. You might want to start students on the activity working in pairs, and as they gain facility, have them form larger cooperative circles of up to eight students.

A variation on the word basket is the number bag, which is good for elementary-level students. Start by grouping students in circles of four to six. The student who goes first—the "number starter"—picks a number under 10 and says it to the student on his or her right ("Six"). That student repeats the number and then throws in an additional number ("Six, four"). The student on his or her right does the same ("Six, four, seven"), and so on. Over time, you can modify the activity to use larger numbers, add processing to the numbers ("Six plus four equals 10" or "Six plus four plus seven equals 17"), or stop and start over after a certain goal is reached. For example, you could instruct students to keep going until the sum reaches 35, or until they have added a certain quantity of numbers from the mental number bag—three or four numbers for younger students, six or seven for older students. As students' skill levels increase, the goals' complexity increases.

Review increasingly large chunks of content. This review method, which gradually increases the amount and complexity of content reviewed, builds strong attentional and listening skills and working memory. Like the word basket and number bag activities, students conduct this activity in groups, taking turns and building on one another's contributions. At the elementary level, place students into groups of three or four and have one group member start by naming a key word or fact related to the content—at first, just a word from the current unit is fine. The student to his or her right repeats the previous word or fact and adds something new, and so on. For example, say the unit is on weather. The first student says "clouds." The next student repeats "clouds" and adds a new word: "humidity." The third student says "Clouds, humidity, barometric." Challenge students to see how far they can go. With practice, they can use this activity to help them build short sentences out of the vocabulary words, or even build paragraphs out of sentences. At this more challenging level, divide students into groups of four or five and ask the first student in each group to start with a short review sentence (fewer than six words) related to the current unit. Each succeeding group member repeats the previous sentences and adds a new one. It might look like this:

Student 1: "The human body has many systems."

Student 2: "The human body has many systems. The respiratory system is an important one."

Student 3: "The human body has many systems. The respiratory system is an important one. The circulatory system keeps blood flowing."

And so on.

You can start using this review method early in the year by teaching new vocabulary words. For example, a science teacher might introduce four new words during the first month of the school year, one each week: *ecology, biodiversity, homeostasis,* and *genetics.* On the first day of week one, he says, "*Ecology* is the science of the relationships between organisms and their environments." Every day that week, he recites the definition, and students repeat it, sometimes practicing with partners. On the first day of week two, he announces, "We are going to repeat last week's word and add a new one for this week: *Ecology* is the science of the relationships between organisms and their environments. *Biodiversity* is the range of variation of species within any environment. Now, let's repeat both sentences." And so on.

Focus on sound. Place K–2 students in groups of three to four. In each group, have one member start by making a sound—an animal sound, a phoneme (e.g., /z/ as in *zoo*), or any other sound relevant to the content—and then toss a ball to another group member. That student repeats the previous sound, adds a new one, and then tosses the ball to the next person. This activity not only is fun but also engages students physically, which can help improve cognition, and compels them to pay attention, thus building their listening skills and working memory.

Consider having younger students sing any of a number of songs that are excellent for building working memory. The lyrics in songs like "Old MacDonald Had a Farm" and "The 12 Days of Christmas" keep building on themselves and motivate students to keep track of all the previous verses.

Use a quick fix. When you're seriously pressed for time, integrate a short-term solution into the lesson. Before initiating an activity, announce the directions and then have students repeat them to a neighbor or partner. This way, you're reinforcing working memory while not taking any time away from the lesson.

Action #4: Develop Processing Speed

Processing generally refers to the act of working with or modifying something. When students are processing, they are doing mental work. Mental processing includes a broad category of skills (e.g., collecting, sorting, summarizing, calculating, organizing, and analyzing) that are all teachable. In fact, these skills *must* be taught; they are not innate skills.

Our brains engage in processing at both macro and micro levels. At the macro level, processing could mean dealing with anything from a difficult relationship to self-esteem issues. In an academic context, a teacher might foster macro-processing by having students read a story about a character who gets in trouble and then asking students, "How would you deal with this situation?" At the micro level, students' brains are continually altering tiny bits of information. For example, with auditory processing, students need to learn how to distinguish between words like *watch* and *wasp* or *boys* and *buoys,* or they'll struggle with phonemes, the essential building blocks of reading.

Low-SES students are more likely than their higher-SES peers to have auditory processing and language deficits (Noble, Norman, & Farah, 2005). We can help students who struggle with these processing issues; there is no reason why students should be unable to read by 3rd grade. A host of intervention programs can help develop reading skills, including READ 180, Open Court Reading, Lindamood-Bell, Lexia Reading, Wilson Reading System, Failure Free Reading, and SpellRead. You may also want to try an auditory processing software program, such as Fast ForWord or Reading Assistant, both of which are based on solid brain research (Temple et al., 2003; Thibodeau, Friel-Patti, & Britt, 2001). When targeted at the right population and well implemented, computer-based programs not only develop processing speed but also build working memory and attention.

Reading, writing, and math calculation need to be taught. Even when taught well, learning these processes often takes months of practice. When students process a story, they are engaging in a host of mental activities, including predicting, analyzing, and summarizing. These all provide superb engagement possibilities. The section that follows introduces quick, active processing activities. You can find more detailed engagement strategies for teaching processing skills in grades 4–12 in the book *Deeper Learning* (Jensen & Nickelsen, 2008).

Solutions You Can Use

Have students "show and shout." This activity helps teach math processing skills. Have students form circles of three to five students and stand facing their group mates. On your cue ("Ready, SHOW, count, and SHOUT!"), each student flings out his or her hand, showing between zero and five fingers. Then each student tallies the fingers shown in his or her group (e.g., 2 + 3 + 1 + 4 + 5) and shouts out the total ("15!"). Whoever is first wins. You can vary the activity's complexity by having students multiply the numbers, put them in sequence, or do any other sort of calculation. Younger students could line up in order, from greatest to smallest number. Older students can show two hands—one high and one low, to represent the numerator and the denominator of a fraction—and, again, line up in order from greatest to smallest. To train working memory, ask students to hide their hands back behind their backs and then recall who had which numbers. To build fluency and processing speed in math, gradually speed up the activities with either a deadline or fast-paced instrumental background music.

Make body angles. This is another activity good for building math processing skills. Stand in front of the class, announce an angle (say, 45°), and wait for students to bend their bodies to that angle. Next, have a student come up front to call out an angle. You can vary this activity by calling out additional shapes or objects that students can represent physically.

Create a learning list. This activity helps with language arts processing. You can divide up the content and allow students (with partners, in a group, or on a team) to select a passage or chapter from a text or a whole story. Then have them develop lessons for the text, creating a list of (1) key ideas or characters; (2) questions to build comprehension; (3) comments about the content (e.g., its themes or aspects that held personal meaning); and (4) things that puzzle, intrigue, or need clarification. At this point, students share their learning lists with their partners, fellow group members, or teammates. Some may also volunteer to present their work to the class.

Scramble stories. Post (or have a student post) a four- or five-sentence paragraph in the front of the classroom, with the sentence order scrambled. Give students five minutes to rewrite the paragraph, putting the sentences into their logical sequence. Then have students share their revised paragraphs with partners, justifying why they put each sentence where they did.

Use posted models. Posted models help students practice and internalize processes. For language arts, post the steps of the writing process, and for math, post the steps for problem solving. You can even post steps to teach appropriate behaviors and social skills. For example, low-SES students are more likely than their higher-SES peers to experience chronic stress, so without singling out any students, consider posting the following steps:

How to Deal with My Stress

- Take action if appropriate (e.g., talk to the person who is agitating you, or brainstorm solutions for your own problem).

- Write down what is stressing you and what action you will take later.

- Use mental relaxation tools like positive self-talk, slow breathing, and meditation.

- Release the stress. Use the one-week rule: if what you're stressed about won't matter in one week, let it go.

- Work it off with exercise, chores, or play.

After posting the steps, use the same modeling and scaffolding process explained on page 59: model and explain the steps, provide time for guided practice (e.g., have students use the steps to deal with a hypothetical scenario), review how students did and correct errors, and then foster independent practice. Practice these steps with students every week. They will not only empower students to deal more capably with damaging stress but also build cognitive capacity.

Action #5: Foster Self-Control

The famous Stanford marshmallow experiment provides an interesting example of self-control. The young subjects of the experiment were told that they could have one small reward immediately or two small rewards if they waited until the experimenter returned after an absence of about 15 minutes. The children who most successfully delayed gratification demonstrated higher social competence, academic success, and personal efficacy in their teenage years (Mischel, Shoda, & Rodriguez, 1989). The benefits even persisted into their adult years (Casey et al., 2011).

Self-control is an immensely valuable skill that supports thinking, learning, and decision making, yet it is rarely taught. Children raised in poverty in particular tend to have greater impulsivity, which leads to behavioral issues (Razza, Martin, & Brooks-Gunn, 2012). Students cannot exert self-control unless they can also exercise the skills of *prioritization, prediction,* and *inhibition.* When students plan an essay, select and evaluate paths to solving word problems, choose whether to do homework, or even decide whether to try out for a sport, they are prioritizing. Effective prioritizing fosters the skills of prediction (i.e., the ability to see around corners) and inhibition (i.e., the ability to defer gratification)—but it requires practice, knowledge, and experience. The following section provides some useful activities you can use to develop self-control in your students.

Solutions You Can Use

Use "calendar delays" for classroom question-and-answer time. For this simple strategy, simply let the last digit of the day's date determine the duration of the response delay you give students. For example, if the day of the month ends in a nine (i.e., if it's the 9th, the 19th, or the 29th), when you ask a question, students must count to nine before raising their hands. This practice teaches students to resist their first impulse. Use this strategy with almost any cue, and students will become better at self-regulation.

Teach self-control. Show your class the YouTube video of the Stanford marshmallow experiment, which provides useful clues for self-control that even 5-year-olds can use. The key to the video is observing what the kids who successfully deferred gratification did. Then teach students strategies to use in situations that require self-control, such as waiting in line. For example, students can keep busy with active distracter tasks like clapping, stretching, and counting; use positive self-talk to tell themselves that they have the power to choose to do the right thing; or remind themselves of the rewards of self-control ("If I am calm and wait quietly, I'll get to eat earlier than if I am disruptive").

Use reverse active cues. For example, in the clapping task, instruct students to clap twice when you clap once, and to clap once when you clap twice. After some practice, lead a series of mixed one-clap and two-clap trials. Over time, add more complexity; for example, when you clap three times, students clap twice. This task trains students to inhibit their immediate impulses or desires and replace them with the fresh alternative responses in working memory.

Teach the power of micro-goals. Start by telling students the next task they'll be engaging in—choosing a partner for an activity or taking a short walk within the classroom, for example. Then ask students to set a mental goal to wait for just 10 seconds before starting on the task. Most students can do that easily. As soon as the 10 seconds are up, ask them to wait for 10 *more* seconds. Teach them wait strategies, such as closing their eyes, redirecting their energy, or entertaining themselves. This micro-goal strategy helps students learn how to go about reaching their own personal goals in small chunks. They learn that at any time, on any day of their lives, they have the ability to wait for few more seconds or minutes for something that's worthwhile.

"Unstick" Your Thinking

Although students are not stuck with the cognitive capacity they have, some teachers are stuck in their thinking. So when a teacher laments, "These kids can't seem to learn," my response is, "What are you doing to build their capacity?" If your students are not high performers, are you going to complain about it and then lower your expectations? Or are you going to give them a real shot at success?

It's time to stop telling students what to do and start teaching them *how to do it*. Then have them practice it repeatedly over time. Average teachers teach a skill until students get it right; highly effective teachers work with students until they can't get it wrong. Forget about kids not being "school-ready." *All* humans are born with only rudimentary cognitive skills. If your students are lagging, teach them and help them hone these core skills, and they will be much more likely to succeed in school and in life.

5

Engage for Motivation and Effort

> ### The Connecting Engagement Factors
>
> - **Effort and energy:** Motivational and effort-building strategies increase effort and energy by making learning relevant, awakening curiosity and enthusiasm, affirming students' capacity, and encouraging student participation and positive risk taking.
> - **Mind-set:** Motivational and effort-building strategies positively shape students' attitudes about learning, foster a growth mind-set, and create mind-body states that are receptive to feedback and further learning.
> - **Cognitive capacity:** Motivational and effort-building strategies reinforce students' belief that their cognitive capacity is not fixed and build the capacity to learn even more.
> - **Relationships:** Motivational and effort-building strategies build an inclusive, positive class climate and strengthen the class's social glue.
> - **Stress level:** Motivational and effort-building strategies manage risk and strengthen students' locus of control to increase their self-efficacy, strengthen the body's stress response, and develop greater resilience and long-term effort.

In the Classroom

Brittany has taught 5th grade at a Title I elementary school for two years. When she asks her class for questions or suggestions, students remain passive. One or two hands may go up, but most stay down. In addition, her adequate yearly progress scores are down in math and language arts. As she sees it, her students have "motivation problems. They just sit there. They don't take notes, they're slow to interact, and my attempts at cooperative learning have been a disaster." Recently, she concluded that "these kids just don't want to learn." She's not even sure she wants to stay in teaching; her biggest reason for remaining is the slow job market. The minute another job opens up, she'll be gone.

At the same school, Ron has taught 4th grade for almost 20 years. A visit to his class reveals his obvious passion for teaching. Ron loves his kids. That's what he calls them: "my kids." He will not let any student fail—at anything. And students actually want to be in his class every day! Student motivation and effort seem to come easy here.

But the key to Ron's success isn't that he is a "natural" or that he lucked out with a group of star pupils. After observing Ron in action, it's clear why students in his class are engaged, holding their hands high and hoping to get called on. Ron gives every single student he calls on his full attention. He offers a smile and nod of acknowledgment and a verbal affirmation of the student's contribution. In short, Ron has mastered the skill of affirming what he values: engagement.

Five Actions to Increase Motivation and Effort

If I asked you whether a given student in your class is motivated or lazy, odds are you would have a ready answer. But would that answer be fair or accurate? Before making judgments about students' characters or personalities based on their supposed level of effort, hold up a mirror to your own practice. Ask yourself, how much effort have *you* made in the last year to upgrade your own knowledge, skills, and passion? How many resources on engagement have you read and applied? How often have you gone the extra mile to build strong relationships with your students? How many engagement strategies have you tried and tweaked over the last year? If you find these questions difficult or uncomfortable to answer, this chapter is for you.

Let's drop the myth that there are unmotivated students. We all go in and out of numerous mind-body states throughout the day. In some, we feel motivated and engaged, and in others, we don't. You and I feel unmotivated at times, but that does not make us unmotivated people. So why would we slap such a black-and-white, judgmental label on a student? There is no such thing as an unmotivated student; there are only students in unmotivated states, sitting in demotivating classrooms. Notice how high schoolers participate strongly in some classes but are disconnected in others. Same kids, different teachers. Successful teachers make schoolwork interesting, and they influence students' states so that students are ready to learn. When it comes to student motivation and behavior, quality of instruction is a much stronger influence than is students' purported character.

Although genetics have some small connection to motivated, reward-seeking behaviors (Persson et al., 2000), some drivers contributing to effort and motivation are learned, and others are environmental (e.g., family, friends, work, culture, school, and life circumstances). If a learning environment is boring and irrelevant, students will see no reason to put in any effort. If students live in poverty or other adverse circumstances, they are even more likely to feel a lack of motivation. Although students across all socioeconomic levels experience unmotivated states, low-SES students are more likely to exhibit either hyperactivity or disconnectedness as a result of acute or chronic stressors. These symptoms of stress disorders can all too easily be misinterpreted as acting out or lethargy. Instead of taking such behavior as an affront, take the time to understand the human beings behind the behaviors. If you don't, the odds of engaging these students will drop precipitously.

This chapter provides engagement strategies that will help you continually, meaningfully activate students' motivation to learn. As motivation to learn increases, so too do curiosity and the capacity to learn even more. You will learn how to get students to *want* to contribute more in class. This is not some esoteric quest; you simply need to understand what drives students to work hard. This chapter lays out five powerful actions you can take to increase student motivation and effort in your own classroom.

Five Actions to Increase Motivation and Effort

1. Make it their idea.
2. Manage risk.
3. Build the learner's mind-set.
4. Provide feedback.
5. Get a trial-size effort.

Action #1. Make It Their Idea

Many kids feel like the world "happens" to them. In psychology, this mind-set is referred to as a low locus of control. When a person is confronted with an adverse situation or person and feels limited control to manage it, his or her brain feels stress. Thus, it makes sense that students who are accustomed to poverty or other adverse circumstances have developed certain coping skills to strengthen their locus of control: if they sense their world getting out of control, they may show anger, helplessness, or both.

Conversely, when perception of control is elevated, stress goes down and learning increases. Black and Deci (2000) found that teacher support of student autonomy correlates positively with academic performance for students initially low in self-regulation. When it comes to student achievement, having a sense of control has, on average, a moderate effect size of 0.30 (Patall, Cooper, & Robinson, 2008; Patall, Cooper, & Wynn, 2010). The effect increases with students living in poverty, because they start from a higher baseline of stress (Evans & Kim, 2012).

Here's the upshot: to increase your students' locus of control and, by extension, their engagement and learning, let them make more choices. When you give students a choice, they are more likely to give something a try. You don't need to cede control of your class, or even offer students particularly significant choices. The *feeling* of having some control is at least as important as actually having control. For this reason, it's essential to "sell" a choice so that students are aware of the power they're being given. For example, it's less effective to say, "On our next assignment, you can either work alone or with a partner. Go ahead and begin." To drive home the fact that you're handing students the reins, say, "I bet you'd like to decide whether to work alone or with a partner on our next assignment. So I'm letting you have it your way: *you* get to choose!"

If you're hesitant to let students take more control, keep in mind that you don't lose power by giving it away; there's no "power pie" with only so many slices. In fact, the more you share power in the classroom, the bigger the pie gets—and the happier and more empowered your students will be. Every time I visit or read about high-performing teachers, the pattern is the same: they engage with ownership, purpose, and collaboration. The following section provides specific strategies you can use to give students a sense of control.

Solutions You Can Use

Provide content choice. When appropriate, provide students with a choice of content ("Do you want to learn about this aspect of the topic or that one?"); social conditions ("Who would rather work with a neighbor on this assignment?"); or learning process ("You have three choices to gather information for this assignment: research online sources, watch and consult these DVDs, or conduct an in-person interview"). Remember to sell the choice!

Middle school teacher Whitney Henderson teaches English in New Orleans, in one of the poorest neighborhoods you could imagine. Yet she typically propels her students to make two to three years of academic gains for every school year they attend. She gets these astounding results by giving students relevant choices and making deliberate connections between the content she teaches and the lives of her students. She helps students uncover their dreams, invites them to write about those dreams, and then helps them make their dreams come alive. In Whitney's classroom, kids don't write just to complete an assignment; they are writing to solve real community problems and to understand others' viewpoints while communicating their own.

Let students run a "Classroom City." Classroom City is an educational product that helps students develop responsibility, thinking skills, and initiative. The program has students design, run, and sustain a simulated city in their classroom over the course of up to 30 class periods. All class members have real-world jobs (e.g., mayor, firefighter, teacher) that replicate those found in a modern city. The students plan the city's geographical and political structure, elect officials, appoint individuals to city positions, and learn to earn and manage money. Students are engaged every day, because they all have roles to play.

Hold regular "drumroll drawings." Sometimes small things can become engaging classroom rituals. Here's one: write all of your students' names on cards or paper slips and keep them in a bowl or another container. At any point during class, let one student come up to the container and draw out two student names (the name draw-er is ineligible). Have students do a drumroll on their desks for added suspense. One of the two students chosen gets a standing ovation (pure fun!), and the other gets to answer a student-submitted question related to the unit of study. Have students submit questions in advance, and vet them before using them.

Delegate tasks with classroom jobs. This may be the simplest way to engage students and give them some control over the class's proceedings. At the elementary level, "hire" a materials handler to pass out and collect supplies; an environmental agent to manage lighting, temperature, windows, and plants; and a security officer to be a line leader or line ender. At the secondary level, you'll need illustrators to write down student suggestions and create visual aids, graphic organizers, and posters for the class; a special effects manager to act as class DJ, do drum rolls on the desk, or be in charge of a punctuating instrument like a tambourine or drum; and "energy directors" to lead the class in short dance moves and stretch breaks or simply signal the teacher when energy lags. Share the power so that students feel some ownership of the class and its proceedings. Chapter 8 discusses classroom jobs in further depth.

Have students write the rules. Ask students to contribute ideas for class rules or consequences through classroom discussions, and follow through by having them vote or submit ideas in a suggestion box. Each week, give students a few minutes to add to the suggestion box, and have selected students take turns doing the job of reading and sorting suggestions and tallying votes. Again, this requires a power-sharing mentality in which you ask yourself, "How can I expect to keep kids invested in the process if I don't give them a piece of the action?"

Encourage students to become mentors. Mentoring others can provide students with a sense of control over their lives, build dependable relationships, and help both mentors and mentees with academics. Some very successful mentoring programs bring students from one to two grade levels higher to work with struggling students for a half-hour after school. But you can also set up in-class mentoring.

Leslie Ross teaches biology in a low-income high school in Greensboro, North Carolina. On the first day of school, she asks her students, "Who thinks they can get an *A* or a *B* in my course?" After some students raise their hands, she says, "Great. But can you help someone else get an *A*, too?" She asks each student to submit the names of two classmates—his or her top two choices to be a study buddy—and then assigns the partnerships. Each pair of study buddies exchanges phone numbers, shares materials, cheers each other on, competes for class awards, and sits together. Leslie tells her students, "If you get a perfect score and your buddy fails, you both have failed." In her high-performing class, stronger students tutor their struggling partners, and buddies support and even pressure their partners to complete their work. The results speak for themselves: her biology students, on average, outscored all other students on districtwide assessments by more than 25 percentage points.

Engage students in project learning. Project learning—the time-honored teaching approach of having students learn authentically by working on real-world projects and challenges—requires the skills of planning, prioritizing, risk management, and decision making. Students need to keep the project's ultimate goal in mind while managing resources, time, and people. For example, for a unit on weather in an upper-elementary classroom, a four-student cooperative group might research, script, and produce a video weather forecast. At the secondary level, projects may include setting up a schoolwide recycling program, creating a "Respect Your Classmates" anti-bullying campaign, or fund-raising for a student-determined cause. The students are the ones who generate these projects and make the important choices along the way, and the resulting sense of ownership ensures that they continually put in strong effort and remain highly engaged.

Have students self-assess. Self-assessment is a strong strategy to help students reflect on and improve their learning. One way to foster effort is to invite student input in developing rubrics, and empower students to use them to assess their own learning and progress. The process of self-assessment develops students' sense of mastery and control over their learning.

Jamie Irish, the 8th grade teacher who challenges his students to outscore a nearby school, posts the competitor school's scores at the front of the room, breaking them down into the four levels of proficiency: Advanced, Mastery, Basic, and Unsatisfactory. He breaks down his own class's results from each test into those same levels of proficiency and displays them, too. He teaches students how to analyze data, evaluate their scores, and set actionable goals for the next test. In this way, he transfers ownership of the learning to the students. His students are able to use critical feedback on their progress to set new goals and build a sense of personal accountability.

Action #2: Manage Risk

Students will put more effort into learning when the risk level is low (Treadway et al., 2012). Naturally enough, they want to avoid being mocked by their peers or feeling embarrassed. Before students raise their hands, they must trust that you will never use sarcasm, humiliate them in front of their classmates, or criticize them in a group setting. At any grade level, when students trust you, they will take bigger risks.

Stereotype threat—the risk of reinforcing a negative stereotype about one's group—is a major factor behind many students' unwillingness to take risks and show effort. Steele and Aronson (1995) found that when black college students' race was emphasized before they took a standardized test, they performed worse than white students did. When their race was *not* emphasized before the test, they performed at the same level as white students. These findings tell us that when students believe their behavior might be looked at or judged through the filter of stereotypes, their performance may suffer. Stereotype threat can, of course, hurt the effort and performance of *any* population susceptible to stereotype, including Hispanic students (Schmader & Johns, 2003) and low-SES students (Croizet & Claire, 1998). The strategies in the following section will help you create an environment in which all students feel free to take academic risks.

Solutions You Can Use

Safety first. For students, the rule is simple: respect your classmates. Make clear to students that putdowns and jokes about their classmates' comments or contributions are unacceptable. Remind students with affirmations, a poster, and, most important, your own actions, that their classroom is a safe place to contribute, share, and ask questions. You may also want to lead a discussion about common, damaging stereotypes and prejudices based on ethnicity, religion, or sexual orientation.

For you, the rule is also simple: you must create a safe environment by walking the walk. Always make eye contact, smile, acknowledge the contribution of every single student, and thank students for participating. The less you critique or judge students' contributions, the more hands you'll see going up. Many kids have been put down, embarrassed, or marginalized for years. To elicit student effort, be a shining beacon of positivity in their day. When they raise their hands, make them glad they took the risk.

Role-model the response you want. I often watch teachers—good ones— who ask their class questions with their hands at their sides. It's important to use not only clear directions but also nonverbal cues to tell students exactly *what* you want from them and *how* you expect them to respond. If you expect students to raise their hands and a student calls out an answer instead, he may feel embarrassed and therefore less likely to participate in the future. You can lower student risk by modeling your expectations—by putting your own hand up when you expect students to raise their hands. Accompanying speech with gestures also cues the attentional system, and your students' motor systems will work with their brains' language comprehension areas to determine the meaning of those gestures (Skipper, Goldin-Meadow, Nusbaum, & Small, 2009).

Post and implement participation rules. Set up class rules that clarify your expectations and manage participation risks for students so they're more willing to engage. For example, tell students that participating daily is more than just part of their grade—it's how they learn and grow. To make sure all your students participate actively, post the following rules:

Class Expectations

1. Volunteer a question or comment daily,
2. Respond when called on, or
3. Write out a written content question and give it to me as a "door pass" before you go.

Use "two rounds" for questions. This questioning strategy will increase the level of student participation in your class, help students feel safer and more confident about contributing, and act as a kind of formative assessment, telling you what a large number of students know about a given topic or question. Start by explaining to students that you are going to ask two rounds of questions, the first one a "survey" and the second one reflective.

Round 1

Round 1 questions are quick surveys that require students to give their immediate response and that give you a picture of where your students are in their learning. Start by calling on a student and asking a question. Whether the student's response is correct or incorrect, you should make eye contact, smile sincerely, and thank the student for his or her effort and participation without saying whether the response was right or wrong. Just give a verbal affirmation like "Thanks for contributing," "Love the effort!", "Good enthusiasm; who else has a response?", or "I appreciate your thoughts."

Notice that all of these responses focus on the student's effort, not the content of the answer. In Round 1, never use a "praise word" unless you specifically qualify the word with a mention of effort (e.g., "Good effort!"). Otherwise, the student will be confused ("Hmm . . . did 'Good!' refer to the answer I gave, or the effort I made?"). Students may give inappropriate answers on purpose, just to throw you off balance. Maintain a relaxed attitude, memorize your replies (I have about five that I use, without exception or variation) to avoid being mentally thrown off balance, and remember: Round 1 is all about appreciating students' effort and risk. In that context, all contributions within ethical and tasteful boundaries are acceptable. There are only two types of responses students may make. You can explain them to students like this:

1. **Ready:** When you answer, whether you are right or wrong, you'll be thanked for your effort.
2. **No clue:** Say, "I don't know, but I'd like to know."

When a student doesn't know the answer, say, "Thanks, who's next?" and call on another student. The more students you call on during Round 1, the more you find out about what the class knows and doesn't know. Make sure to question 50–70 percent of the class, and thank all responders for their effort. Do not evaluate, judge, or praise the content of the student answers. The point of this round is to provide critical information about where students stand on the subject being discussed; if students' responses are way off base, you'll need to do some reteaching. It is important to get this information before moving on to Round 2.

Round 2

The reflective nature of Round 2 requires in-depth discussion. Students need to know *how* they know the answer and *why* they think their answer is right, and be ready to extend their answer. Begin Round 2 by asking students to reflect on the responses contributed so far, consulting with a partner or teammates on which response they believe is correct and why. They need to prepare for the next round of questions, which push for deeper, more detailed responses. For example, you may say, "Tell me your thoughts on this topic in more detail, please," or "Let's dig a bit deeper. Why do you say that? How did you come to this answer? Please share what you have on this so far."

When it's time to ask the follow-up questions, invite the whole class to respond, and call on at least three to five students, varying whom you call on. You can use the drumroll drawing method described on page 75 if you like. As with Round 1, there are only two types of responses that students may make:

1. **Ready to contribute:** When you answer, you'll be thanked for both your effort *and* the content of your answer.
2. **Not ready yet; need a lifeline:** You may ask for more time to think or to consult a partner, and the teacher will come back around to check with you soon.

Giving students the opportunity to prepare with classmates makes Round 2 less intimidating than it could be, because they have had time to think and are bolstered by social support. They are less likely to hesitate or feel that they are taking a risk by answering.

Go with the "beat." Speaking out, asking for help, and responding to teacher questions pose a huge risk for your English language learners and minority students who have a comfortable conversational vocabulary at home, but whose academic vocabulary is limited. In addition, many classrooms have peer and cultural issues (e.g., embarrassment among peers that their English is not always clear or easy to understand) that add to participation and engagement barriers (Vandrick, 2000). When your students speak in a nonstandard dialect in class, don't single them out or fault them for it. Continue to affirm their effort to participate ("Thanks so much for jumping in"). If kids feel embarrassed about their dialect or language, they will avoid taking any further risks in class.

It can be helpful to discuss dialects in class as a way of embracing diversity, dispelling both embarrassment and prejudice, and simultaneously reinforcing standard academic language. Begin by explaining that everyone has a "beat." A beat is where an individual feels familiar and at ease. Common beats include Cajun, rural Appalachian, and inner-city dialects. Explain that wherever students grow up—the city, the country, or anywhere in between—affects their beat. Then explain the "school beat." You might say, "A beat isn't bad or good; it's just what you're used to. In school, the one you use will either help or hurt your chances of graduation. Just do your best to use what I model for you. I want to help you succeed."

Ask more inclusive questions. A good way to manage students' risk and encourage them to raise their hands is simply to ask yourself before asking a question, "Is my question inclusive or exclusive?" Exclusive questions automatically eliminate a portion of your students and, in the process, heighten their sense of risk and alienation. Ask these questions often enough, and you'll end up training your own students to disengage.

Make sure at least 80 percent of your questions are inclusive ones that nearly every student is at least *able* to respond to. Pause and think before asking questions that immediately exclude half of your students. Figure 5.1 illustrates the differences between these two types of questions.

Action #3: Build the Learner's Mind-Set

Some students think they're stuck at their present cognitive level. In particular, students who grow up in adverse circumstances like poverty tend to feel less control over their lives, which may result in a sense of hopelessness and low self-efficacy (Ackerman & Brown, 2006). This fixed mind-set is deadly because students are likely to perform at the level where they *believe* they already are, not where they could be. Students' expectation of their grade is a robust predictive factor for achievement (Hattie, 2008), as is their attitude or mind-set about learning (Blackwell et al., 2007). Taken together, these two factors can form either a significant asset or a serious liability. The easy part of teaching is dispensing the content. The hard part is learning how to build or change the mind of every single student. You have far more influence over your students' performance than you may think.

Figure 5.1 Exclusive Questions Versus Inclusive Questions

Exclusive	Inclusive
Who here has ever had the opportunity to travel outside our state?	How many of you would someday like to travel to other states or countries?
Who saw a movie last weekend?	I was thinking of a powerful scene in a movie I just saw. Have you ever had the following experience happen to you?
How many of you completed your homework last night?	How many of you remember that we had homework assigned last night? How many of you meant to do it, but didn't make it happen?
Raise your hand if you've been to the local science museum.	Raise your hand if you've ever seen something that just blew your mind.

According to Carol Dweck, author of *Mindset* (2006), the way a teacher talks to students greatly affects how students shape their mental models of their own capacity. Dweck points out that subtle conversations can actually change students' effort levels. Some well-meaning teachers inadvertently lower their students' engagement and subsequent achievement through what researchers call "comfort talk." These teachers think they're doing struggling students a favor when they say things like

- "It's all right. Maybe you're just one of those students who isn't good at math."
- "Bless your heart; you really mean well."
- "That's OK; you can be good at other things."

These well-intended comments actually hurt students' performance (Rattan, Good, & Dweck, 2012). The lowered expectations, easily perceived by students, decrease motivation and, ultimately, effort. To succeed with all students—especially those living in poverty or other adverse circumstances—teachers need to be on a daily mission to build attitude, effort, capacity, and behavior. Don't make excuses or try to make students feel artificially better for doing poorly. Instead, focus on students' capacity to grow and change, and emphasize where they have control over their learning. Teachers influence student beliefs every day. Simple affirmations that steer students' thinking toward a learner's mind-set can have a lasting payoff.

Solutions You Can Use

Affirm students' ability to learn. It is important to reinforce students' belief that their cognitive capacity is not fixed—that new learning can change the brain. Go ahead: tell students explicitly, in plain English, "Your brain can change!" Avoid using words like *talented* or *gifted*, which imply that cognition or ability is static and out of their control. And remember that it is so much better to be blunt than to use comfort talk: "I'm sorry that these concepts are tough for you. You may have not been prepared well enough for this level of math, and that's too bad. But you really can learn these concepts and become skilled at this. I'll do everything I can to help you get caught up and succeed."

Affirm students' trust in you. When you give students a reason to trust in you, they'll work harder. One award-winning teacher says bluntly to her students, "You are in the presence of an awfully good teacher. I have the skills and expertise to help you succeed. I will guide you through the process; just do what I ask, and you'll get an *A* or a *B*." During the first week of school, one of her students blurted out, "What if I do all of that, and I still fail?" The teacher replied, "That's never happened! If you do all that I ask, then you won't fail" (Wu, 2012, p. 17).

Successful teachers exude a contagious confidence. Do you have that level of confidence in yourself? If you do, share it with your students. Tell them, "You will succeed. Just show up, follow my lead, put in a big effort, and you'll succeed." Kids need relentless enthusiasm from you. Can you "bring it" every day?

Affirm students' choices, attitudes, and effort. The three big attributes of learning that are in students' control are (1) their choices of learning or problem-solving strategies; (2) their attitudes; and (3) their level of effort. Use the dozens of daily teacher-student interactions you have as teachable moments that affirm these factors:

- *Affirm students' choices:* "I love how you kept trying so many strategies on that math problem until you got it."

- *Affirm students' attitudes:* "Before you began, you knew you could succeed. I admire that optimistic, positive attitude." And, "We *all* experience setbacks. Never be afraid to fail. We will all fail at one time or another. It's what we do *after* the failure that determines our success. Do you get up off the floor after the failure, learn from your mistakes, and charge ahead? That's what will make you successful in the long run."

- *Affirm students' effort:* "When you took on that challenging project, you must have known it was going to be a lot of work. You had to plan your steps, organize your resources, get help, and create a high-quality product. You did all that, and I think you're going to learn a lot in school."

Affirm students' capacity. Students who believe that they have unlimited reserves of focus, effort, and willpower try harder over the long haul than do those who think such resources are finite (Job, Dweck, & Walton, 2010). Avoid communicating to students that their capacity to learn is limited. Avoid planting negative thoughts with statements like "I know it's late in the afternoon, and you're probably brain-dead by now, but let's just try to do this last activity." Don't reinforce how tired students look or how hot it is, or how their effort has dropped. If you tell students their attention span is only five minutes long, many will mentally bog down after four to five minutes. The relationship between effort expended and classroom motivation and cognition is strong (Job et al., 2010). To build resilience, affirm students' capacity to sustain effort over the long haul:

- "I know the assignment was a tough one, but you hung in there and got it done. Your nonstop focus, concentration, and effort were awesome!"

- "I like that you refused to give up, even when the task took a lot longer than expected. Remember, failure is only a detour, not the destination. The extra effort you made will help you succeed again and again."

- "Listen, you're putting out an awesome effort, and since that wasn't enough, let's review how you're going about it to see if we can tweak the strategy you're using. I'm confident you'll succeed; we'll just keep making small adjustments until we get it right as a team."

Action #4: Provide Feedback

Kids growing up in poverty typically get less positive feedback at home (Hart & Risley, 1995); in fact, they get 12 times more negative feedback than kids in higher-income homes. The simple act of making feedback available to students—whether it comes directly from the teacher, from the work itself, or from peers—builds effort. Feedback and ongoing formative assessment are in the top 10 of all student achievement factors (Hattie & Timperley, 2007). Although feedback is a powerful motivator, however, it doesn't work well in isolation. For it to reach its full potential of increasing student engagement and effort, teachers must also create challenging learning goals, get student buy-in, give students a sense of control over their learning, and create a positive class climate.

The classic way of giving feedback is to offer a critique or compliment, but research (Deci, Koestner, & Ryan, 1999) has found that praise, punishment, and extrinsic rewards are the least useful forms of feedback. Praise, at least, can positively affect students' attitudes and teacher-student relationships and thus indirectly influence effort. But by far, the most effective forms of feedback provide specific information that *directly* relates to three facets of learning: (1) the learning goal; (2) the amount of progress made toward the goal; and (3) where and how to proceed next. Feedback may simply confirm to students whether they are correct or incorrect, or it may tell them that more information is available or needed. It may also point to alternative strategies to success or open up a new understanding of the learning. Most significantly for the purpose of this book, it invites increased effort, because good feedback moves students closer to their goals, which is highly motivating.

Solutions You Can Use

Use emotional punctuation. This solution first made an appearance in Chapter 3, but it applies here as well. Learn to affirm the little things: "Thanks for taking care of that. I appreciate your thoughtfulness." Or say, "Hey class, if you and your partner finished up on time, give your partner a high five and say, 'We did it!'" This is one of the simplest forms of feedback, but it makes students aware of their growth and leads them to feel confident and receptive to further feedback and learning.

Help students develop and use a rubric. Before developing a rubric, you must clarify the learning goals. Students should be able to define and recognize the specific evidence of goal attainment with absolute certainty. In addition, the feedback provided by the rubric should enable them to measure where they are and decide where to go next. The rubric can be simple. For example, you may want students to use the rubric to look at the following five aspects of goal attainment:

1. Clear statement of all measurable facets of goal
2. Actual progress toward goal
3. Rate of progress
4. Potential obstacles ahead
5. Potential paths or strategies

When students develop and use these analytical skills to assess their own progress, their effort will increase. The feeling of control over their work as well as seeing *how* to reach their goals is very exciting and empowering.

Be clear and constructive. To increase motivation and effort, make sure to strengthen your positive feedback, keep error correction specific and task-oriented, and ask probing questions without criticizing:

- "I love the detail you put in your writing. Please add a bit more of your personal feelings in the details. Let me know what got you excited, scared, stressed, hopeful, or confused. That will help readers feel like they know you better. Adding five or six sentences, sprinkled throughout your story, would make it much stronger."

- "You have a great attitude, and that's something I really admire. I can see you're stuck right now. You might try putting the A/B function on the left side of the equation and working the problem that way. Let me know what happens."

- "Your rubric's got plenty of important detail, which is great. It also suggests you've got a gap to fill in your work. Could you talk to me about that?"

Action #5: Get a Trial-Size Effort

Trial-size products enable consumers to try a product at low risk before making a commitment to buy. You can replicate this model in the classroom. As we know, students—especially low-SES students—tend to be risk-averse in the classroom. But just as consumers who wouldn't normally buy a product outright may be willing to shell out a little money to sample it, students who won't make a huge effort will often make a micro-effort. That small effort might get them only 5 percent of the way toward the goal, but it could be just enough to jump-start a bigger effort. In short, it's much easier to start slow and simple when students are in an unmotivated state than to expect them to go from 0 to 60 all at once.

If students are in a sleepy, grumpy, or unresponsive state, they are unlikely to raise their hands, collaborate actively in groups, or otherwise engage in learning. The solution is to use a multistep process that eases them into the lesson with something fun or quick. Starting with an easy, low-risk activity tweaks students' sluggish mind-body states toward states more conducive to learning and shifts their thinking from "I don't feel like it" to "This might be worth it!"

Solutions You Can Use

Ease students in with "bite-size" moves. To a class of half-asleep students, say, "Before we move on, stamp your feet twice and pound your table twice." Students usually comply (boys especially tend to love this task). Once they're done stamping and pounding, their natural curiosity is awakened, and they wonder, "Why did we do that?" At that split second of curiosity, say, "Please stand up. Take five giant steps. Now, find a partner." With little or no resistance, students have moved from their desks, have paired up with a classmate, and are awake and ready for the next step.

Alternatively, have students begin by stretching their legs out. Then ask them to raise their hands and stretch their arms, too. Next, ask them to lean back, then forward. While students are leaning forward, ask them to push on their knees as hard as they can. Finally, say, "Go ahead and stand up. Now that you're up, please touch the backs of seven chairs and find a partner."

Encourage voluntary hand raising. To get students in the habit of raising their hands, first give them a reason to *want* to raise their hands. A good strategy is to use hand raising as a form of positive recognition. For example, say, "If your neighbor made it to class on time today, raise your hand." The more often you ask students to raise their hands for something that makes sense, has low risk, and feels good, the more comfortable the habit becomes.

Ask students to share opinions. This strategy is an effective setup for having students work in pairs on a lesson-related activity. Say to your class, "Before we go further, turn to your side and tell your neighbor one food you can't stand. [Pause.] Now tell him or her what you are most looking forward to next week. [Pause again.] Now take a moment to compare your class notes and find just one thing they have that you don't have. I'll be asking for your response in two minutes."

Divide content into micro-chunks. When it seems tough to stimulate effort, divide an activity or a reading into manageable micro-chunks that just get students into action. Start by dividing your class into cooperative groups of four or five students and ask them to number off, so each student gets a number between one and five. Then assign a chunk of text or a story and have the groups read it cooperatively. Student number one begins by reading aloud the first sentence, student number two reads the next sentence, and so on. If students' reading skills are weak, simply ask them to identify the subject or the verb in each sentence. At the secondary level, chunk off paragraphs and assign one to each pair. Each pair then reads its paragraph, discusses its meaning, and prepares a summary for the whole class. In this way, a class of 30 students can analyze and summarize a 15-paragraph reading. The point of micro-chunking is to foster participation in any way you can, as often as you can. Once students are more motivated and making an effort, you can increase the length of the text or activity.

Engage and empower with physical responses. Sometimes students get tired of raising their hands. To refresh their energy and increase participation, try having students use a wider range of physical responses to serve as classroom signals. Teach them to use the following cues:

- "If you're ready to do something different, please stand up."
- "Repeat after me for a quick call-and-response activity."

- "Thumbs up if you agree; thumbs down if you disagree."
- "Stomp your feet if you're confused now."
- "Pound the desk if you know this and are ready to move on."
- "Shrug your shoulders if you're lost, and wave your paper if you're not."

When you begin a lesson or activity this way, students are more likely to jump into the next task. Even hard-to-reach students usually respond over time. Let students know you expect them to participate and that you are personally inviting them to plunge right in.

If you want to give students even more agency in the class proceedings, teach them to use different cues to give *you* feedback—for example, to signal when it's time for a stretch break, when the content is getting too heavy, or when the class is going off-course, or to let you know how well you affirmed students during questioning. This helps students feel as though they're exerting some control in helpful ways. In elementary-level classrooms, a teacher aide often fulfills this role, so it's a truly empowering job to give students.

To Get Effort, Make an Effort

When students in your class don't seem to be making a real effort to learn, try to shift your point of view. Consider that students are continually making choices. Every day they ask themselves, "Is participation a good idea? Is this activity worth my effort? Should I bother?" Contrary to popular belief, students don't owe their teachers a thing. Most are in school because the law requires them to be there, and their friends are there.

But you, as a teacher, chose your job. As a teacher, you receive monetary compensation and some degree of emotional or vocational fulfillment in exchange for making your best effort to transform students' lives. Remember, to lay the foundation for sustained motivation and effort in your classroom, you have to build relationships, demonstrate passion, and get buy-in. Only then can you successfully implement the five actions described in this chapter (see Figure 5.2).

Figure 5.2 How to Sustain Motivation and Effort

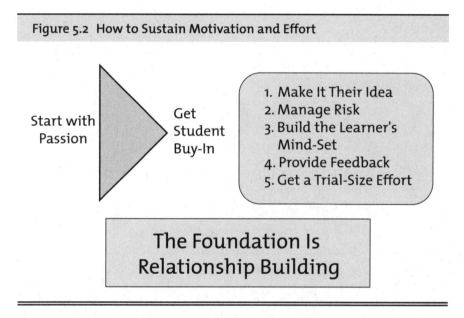

Start with Passion

Get Student Buy-In

1. Make It Their Idea
2. Manage Risk
3. Build the Learner's Mind-Set
4. Provide Feedback
5. Get a Trial-Size Effort

The Foundation Is
Relationship Building

Before you start class every day, decide to make the class worthy of students' effort. Ask yourself if you've done your part and put in the effort to take each of the five actions laid out in this chapter. And remember that showing you care has more of an effect on student motivation than your level of content knowledge. When you yourself are enthusiastic and engaged, your students will feel more excited about learning and will almost always work harder.

6

Engage for Deep Understanding

> **The Connecting Engagement Factors**
>
> - **Vocabulary:** Developing deep representations of knowledge reinforces academic vocabulary, which students can use as the foundation of comprehension to build deeper, increasingly integrated learning.
> - **Effort and energy:** Building deep understanding makes learning richer and more memorable and encourages creativity, leading to increased student enthusiasm and effort.
> - **Cognitive capacity:** Building deep representations of content helps students retain knowledge, transfer it to new contexts, and develop the building blocks needed for more sophisticated levels of comprehension.
> - **Stress level:** Building a deep understanding of knowledge connects students' learning to authentic contexts and empowers them to build meaning independently, increasing their sense of control and decreasing stress.

In the Classroom

Michelle has been teaching 3rd grade for 12 years. She loves her job and cannot imagine doing anything else. Her biggest gripe is simple: "Way too much testing! I have no time for content anymore. It's just gotten out of hand." Michelle feels so overwhelmed that she often resorts to "drill and kill" to make sure she is covering the standards. "Testing has taken the fun out of my job," she laments.

Her best friend, Camilla, also teaches 3rd grade. Camilla runs out of time each day, too, but for a very different reason. Her class is so engaging that everyone loses track of time. Camilla limits her use of worksheets to 10 to 15 minutes a week. To keep students from getting bored, she varies the learning routine from one activity to the next and regularly switches up the learning contexts: sometimes students work individually, sometimes with partners, and sometimes in teams. In addition, her activities vary in complexity and level of challenge: some take only a few minutes to complete, whereas more involved projects may require several weeks.

After a tough day, her frustration boiling over, Michelle confided in Camilla: "My class feels like a factory for test scores. The fun is gone!" Camilla had heard this before. She pulled up her chair, leaned in, and asked, "Michelle, what do you want to have at the end of this school year? Do you want a story about all your grievances, or do you want happy students with high test scores? Do you want excuses or results? I'm serious. About all I hear from you are complaints. Not once have you even asked me for help."

Michelle was caught off guard: "What do you mean?" Camilla said, "Michelle, why have you never asked me *how* I do it? I enjoy my job, I build students' deep understanding of the content while keeping them engaged, and I'm still exceeding AYP. I don't get it; why haven't you asked me how you can do it yourself?"

Michelle thought for a moment. Eventually, she said, "I don't know if I can be like you. I'm just . . . not very creative." Camilla replied, "Look, creativity is not my strong suit, either. I just take a few minutes each day to think about which students I am not reaching and plan some strategies for the next day. I really care about our kids, and I know you do, too. I'd be happy to walk you through what I do and show you how to do it."

Michelle was ready. She said, "It's a deal. Can we meet in your classroom tomorrow after school?"

Five Actions to Build Deep Understanding

The preceding anecdote shows how difficult it can be for teachers to build lasting learning when there are so many other pressing needs to attend to, like testing and classroom management. It also shows that teachers who understand both their content *and* the instructional process have a stronger chance to succeed. Luckily, engagement strategies are good for much more than making school fun for kids; they can help build deep representations of content that stick with students, preparing them not only for tests but also for further learning.

Some teachers believe it's nearly impossible to build these deep representations in the minds of their low-SES students, but this belief is usually based on a misapprehension. When teachers see that low-SES students have smaller academic vocabularies, they often assume that they need to "dumb down" the learning and accordingly end up teaching only surface understandings of labels instead of going for deeper learning. They are operating under the false assumption that students who live in poverty are either unable or unwilling to engage in deeper, more complex learning. Yet highly effective teachers demonstrate repeatedly that low-SES students not only *can* engage in complex learning but also *prefer* it.

Learning can be a complex process. Sometimes it has a clear sequence, and other times it does not. We do know that the brain rarely gets new learning right the first time, unless it is very simple associative learning (e.g., "an apple is a fruit"). Typically, we form rough drafts of new content and hold those drafts until they get either upgraded or dropped (Eichenbaum, 2004). To retain knowledge, connect it with other knowledge to build broader understanding, and transfer it to new contexts, students need to have a deep representation of the content, not just a sloppy surface-level notion of it. Successfully building these deep representations in the brain is a strong factor in student achievement (Hattie, 2003).

Deep representations can develop over time, but building them requires building layers of understanding, meaning, and relevance. The building blocks of deep understanding include a knowledge of labels, an understanding of properties, a grasp of context and meaning, accuracy of understanding, and the ability to transfer the learning (Jensen & Nickelsen, 2008). The first step is understanding labels. These help the brain create markers so that it knows where to store information. The second step is to learn the qualities, or properties, of the labeled content—for example, unique features, essential elements, or compelling assets—to help the brain develop a deeper representation. The third step is to situate the content in some sort of context, and give it appropriate meaning. This is the sense-making part of the process. The fourth step is to ensure accuracy of the understanding through assessment and error correction. The final step, which shows mastery of the content, is typically the learner's ability to connect the understanding to his or her own life or to real-world systems or events. Figure 6.1 shows an example of how this five-step process would help younger students develop an understanding of kangaroos.

Figure 6.1 Five Steps of Building a Deep Representation of *Kangaroo*

1. **Understanding Labels**
   Introduce the subject to students: "This animal is a *kangaroo*."

2. **Discovering Properties**
   Help students identify properties of kangaroos: "Kangaroos have strong legs and tails for jumping. Joeys start in the pouch."

3. **Developing Context and Meaning**
   Bring the class to the zoo or show them the movie *Joey*. Ask students to describe their own impressions of or experiences with kangaroos.

4. **Getting It Right**
   Have students create and exchange quizzes about kangaroos, then take them and discuss results.

5. **Learning to Transfer**
   Discuss: "Do you think the invention of hands-free baby carriers, fanny packs, or pogo sticks was inspired by kangaroos' properties?"

This chapter lays out five actions connected to these core building blocks that will help your students develop deep, sustained understanding.

Five Actions to Build Deep Understanding

1. Understand labels.
2. Discover properties.
3. Develop context and meaning.
4. Get it right.
5. Learn to transfer.

Action #1: Understand Labels

Labels are the "what" of learning. The brain needs a name for content so that it can store it and retrieve it in the future. Learning labels is superficial yet very important: it kick-starts the process of understanding. Even 2-year-olds seem to be competent at registering and mapping labels quickly, suggesting this is a core language competency (Spiegel & Halberda, 2011). Researchers (McDonough, Song, Hirsh-Pasek, Golinkoff, & Lannon, 2011) think we learn noun-labels first because they are easier to imagine. For example, noun-labels related to weather include *tornado, cloud, rain, hurricane,* and *snow*—all words that are easy to visualize. Yet children raised in poverty tend to have a poorer grasp of labels, connected to their smaller vocabularies, which puts them behind their peers when they start school (Hart & Risley, 1995). The following strategies will help you develop students' ability to learn these key labels.

Solutions You Can Use

Informally assess students' prior knowledge of the terms in your upcoming unit. Prior knowledge can be either helpful or harmful to the learning process. Assessing students' prior knowledge of the content will tell you what they already know, what gaps they need to fill, and any misconceptions they have. One way to do this is to have students work with partners to brainstorm words they know about the topic (say, weather). Then ask them to write out statements using the words they brainstormed (e.g., "Tornadoes happen in warm climates"). Alternatively, you could give students a short word-association quiz. Generate a list of 10 to 20 labels related to the new content and ask students to tell you what they already know about the key terms.

Both the statements and the informal quiz will provide essential guidance on how to proceed in your teaching. The most likely scenario is that you'll need to build up your students' vocabulary. Make it a daily priority; Carleton and Marzano's (2010) *Vocabulary Games for the Classroom* is a good resource to consult.

Connect their labels with other labels. Students need to learn new labels that are associated with the labels they already know to develop further "hooks" for learning. Take five minutes to introduce a chunk of content to the class, and then introduce the content's key ideas and labels. Then divide students into small groups and have each group create a list, through word association, of every label they can think of that connects to the original word.

For example, let's go back to weather-related labels like *tornado, cloud, rain, hurricane,* and *snow.* For this activity, students will pick just one label from the list—say, *tornado*—and generate as many associated labels as they can. These may include *wind, damage, buildings, disaster, injuries,* and *fear.* Students can support one another's recall of labels through discussion: "That makes me think of . . ." or "I was also thinking of this word because . . . ."

Next, have groups mix with other groups to add to their lists, eventually creating a master list of labels generated by the whole class that will jump-start their learning of the content. This activity begins to develop the larger pool of labels that underlie a piece of expert knowledge.

Capture the essentials. Instead of lamenting that students have poor memory, give them real tools they can use to retain the content. Teach them mnemonic devices such as associations, peg words, or acronyms. Using simple acronyms can bolster students' knowledge of labels in the content they're studying, which gives them confidence. For example, in a science class, teach students the taxonomic ranks for biological classification (Kingdom, Phylum, Class, Order, Family, Genus, Species) with the mnemonic sentence "Kids Prefer Cheese Over Fresh Green Spinach." Or for a lesson on geography or economics, you could teach students the real-life acronyms that economists use to refer to the most economically volatile European countries ("PIGS" for Portugal, Italy, Greece, and Spain; you may want to note that some find this acronym offensive) and to newly economically advanced countries ("BRIC" for Brazil, Russia, India, and China).

Action #2: Discover Properties

Properties, the defining features of the content being learned, build on labels to create a deeper layer of understanding. For instance, when students are learning about weather, they must develop an understanding of the properties of such labels as *snow.* Snow is cold, wet, and white. It can also be granular, flaky, chunky, or powdery. Snow formation requires the temperature to be at or below the freezing level. Above freezing, snow melts back into water. Snow can fall gently or be driven by strong winds as a blizzard. The label *snow* alone will not tell us what makes snow *snow*. But knowing these properties helps students begin to understand the label and to make key distinctions between it and other labels. The following strategies will help you teach students the process of discovering properties.

Solutions You Can Use

Have students organize their existing content labels. Have students analyze labels and group them in lists or graphic organizers, such as bubble maps, according to categories they have come up with. This grouping process drives learners to ask themselves important analytical questions like, "Why would this label go with that one?"

Using the topic of weather, for example, students may come up with groupings like "events" (including labels like *tornado, flood,* and *storm*); "clouds" (including labels like *cirrus, fog,* and *alto*); "winds" (including labels like *trades, prevailing, Santa Ana,* and *nor'easter*); and "snow" (including labels like *freezing, precipitation, white,* and *flakes*). This process leads students to identify different labels' common features—their properties.

After grouping the labels, students can tease out some of the labels' properties by asking and answering a series of questions about each label. Here are some sample questions for the label *snow:*

1. What is always true about snow?
2. How does snow affect people's health, cars, and jobs?
3. What are some good and bad things about snow?
4. What makes snow different from other weather events?

These questions help students begin to link properties with labels and thus deepen their comprehension of the content they're studying. For example, one answer to question 3 might be, "Snow can freeze over for sledding, skiing, or ice skating. It can be clumpy enough to make snowballs or a snowman." Notice how these questions help students pull some of the defining qualities, or properties, from the label *snow*. The better the quality of the questions, the more properties students can uncover.

Odd Word Out. Once students have created groups of labels and properties, it's time for an activity called "Odd Word Out." Ask each student to add one word to a group of labels that does not belong. Then have students pair up and quiz their partners on the odd word out. If students understand the labels, they should be able to identify which labels fit in the grouping—and which label is not like the others.

Review and strengthen properties. This activity reinforces students' understanding of the connection between labels and their properties, and you can use it in any subject area. In language arts, the labels could be parts of speech or even punctuation marks. For example, students could physically express the property of an exclamation point—emphasis or excitement—by jumping up and down. In chemistry class, the teacher could use elements' names as labels: whenever students hear a given name and atomic number, they respond by shouting out the name of the element and physically demonstrating the property of its form. For example, in response to "Number 1," they would shout, "Hydrogen!" and move their arms outward to indicate a gas. They could indicate liquid elements by making waves with their hands and solid elements by smacking a fist into an open hand.

Analyze the properties that make a label unique. This activity helps students process the distinctions among different labels, or concepts, in a lesson. Ask students to draw two columns on a piece of paper. Then, in the left column, students create a list of new vocabulary terms (labels) from the current unit; in the right column, they generate a list of properties that belong to the labels. Working with a partner, they then scramble the order of the lists and create a quiz that requires the quiz taker to match each label in the left column with its corresponding property in the right column. Each pair exchanges its quiz with another pair and takes the quiz. The goal of this activity is to develop an accurate and fast response and establish the building blocks needed for more sophisticated levels of comprehension to come later.

Then have students express their understanding of the different concepts in a written summary. For example, if you were teaching a lesson about the three branches of the U.S. government, students would identify properties that distinguish each branch from the others (e.g., "headed by the president" for executive, "passes laws" for legislative, and "headed by the Supreme Court" for judicial), and then write a paragraph describing each branch and explaining its defining properties.

Let students teach one another. Peer teaching is a core engagement strategy used to build students' comprehension of content. It's helpful to vary the format, so students stay fresh and engaged in the process. You might ask students to do any of the following:

• Summarize a lesson in five bullet points. Each bullet point consists of a label that prompts the student to recall the related properties. Each student gets a few minutes to revise or check their bullet points for accuracy. Then students pair up, and each partner teaches the other about the topic using the bullet points.

• Make a list of three properties about a key term or concept and then "sell" a partner on why the term or concept is so important to learn, using only the properties to bolster their argument. This activity reinforces that it's not a concept's *label* that makes it important; it's the concept's *properties* that really explain it. For example, a student might say, "The Supreme Court [key concept] has the authority to overturn laws and influence public policy about many things you care about, such as gun control, abortion, same-sex marriage, and immigration." The eventual goal is to be able to synthesize and share the most important properties of the term in 20 seconds.

• Take a position on a controversial issue (e.g., voting rights for convicted felons) and debate it with a partner. The "pro" student would argue in favor of voting rights, whereas the "con" student would argue against voting rights. The debate must center on properties—of felons (e.g., the extent to which felons have a stake in our country, whether they count as citizens, and what citizenship guarantees) and voting (e.g., the various locations where voting should be able to take place, what qualifies a person for the right to vote, whether everyone should have a say in each election). When students focus on properties, the debate ends up being deeply rooted in core issues rather than based on who talks faster or louder or tells the most interesting personal story.

- Choose two labels, such as *hurricane winds* and *tornado winds,* or *two-legged mammals* and *four-legged mammals,* and generate properties for each. Then students compare and contrast the properties of each label with a partner. Next, each pair groups with another pair and shares its findings.

Action #3: Develop Context and Meaning

If labels put a name to the learning, and properties tell us the distinctive features of the learning, then context and meaning constitute the heart and soul of the learning. These qualities situate the learning in a mental environment —cognitive, spatial, historical, or emotional. Context lends learning a shape that makes it much richer than just a label. You can deliver a lecture on meteorological phenomena, but having students in your class recount real stories of their own encounters with scary weather makes the learning much more relevant and memorable. Together, context and meaning help assign to a chunk of learning the values that are needed to build long-term buy-in, memory, and relevance. The strategies that follow will help you make content come alive and stick with students.

Solutions You Can Use

Make it personal. Give students a chance to share personal stories that connect to the topic you're introducing. You can have them engage in a short writing activity, relate stories verbally with partners or in small groups, or tell their stories to the whole class. This strategy has the potential to reinforce the content in ways you never dreamed of. Imagine the power of a riveting weather survival story told by a student: the whole class will be hooked, and the learning will be all the more indelible.

Many kids from low-income homes have not had the exposure to books, museums, or travel that would help them connect with texts. Many kids from middle- and upper-income homes have not had the life experiences that kids from poverty have had. Your students' life experiences are a rich source of background knowledge and potential narrative strategy for you to tap in your classroom. Letting students tell their own stories, in appropriate formats, makes for riveting drama and affirms to students that they're not alone in their life experiences.

Generate and test hypotheses. Students often have intuitions, beliefs, and experiences connected to the content we teach. You can honor their points of view while building meaning by having them work in teams to generate hypotheses about why something is the way it is, or simply about how something works. Have each team pick the hypothesis from its list that is most conducive to being tested in a classroom. Next, ask teams to come up with critical questions about their hypotheses. They can then explore those questions by designing an experiment to test them, creating a problem addressing the question and determining success criteria for solving it, or conducting factual or historical research and analysis.

A simple but relevant experiment would be to test products that students see or use regularly—hand sanitizer, for example. Many parents worry about germs and tell their kids to use hand sanitizer frequently. Students could design a simple science experiment around the hypothesis that washing their hands is as effective as using hand sanitizer.

Teach vocabulary daily. A word-of-the-day activity can be a fun way to teach and reinforce new vocabulary. Have students select a new word to learn from a posted list of vocabulary words to give them a sense of control. To strengthen context and meaning, ask students to

- Use the word in a conversation with a fellow student.
- Create a question about the word that their partner must answer.
- Create synonyms and antonyms for the word and compare results with classmates to arrive at the most accurate ones.
- Create a simile or metaphor for the word.
- Illustrate the word in a drawing or collage.
- Define the word in the context of a story.
- Connect the word to their own lives or to the world at large.

Make sure to rotate these activities so that students' learning stays fresh. You might offer some kind of incentive for using the new word; for example, give students who correctly use the new word in class a pass to leave first at the end of class, or enter them into a drawing for lunch with you.

Deepen the meaning with brief writing tasks. This activity helps students develop a strong sense of meaning. First, divide students into teams of four to six. Each team member begins by writing a four- to eight-sentence summary of the content learned in the preceding half-hour. After five minutes, have students stop writing and pass their summaries to the student on their right. Then each student gets 90 seconds to read his or her neighbor's summary and write a brief comment on it as a form of peer edit. The comment can focus on any quality you choose to emphasize: content accuracy, sentence construction, clarity, or grammar, for example. After the initial peer review, the students once again pass the papers to their right and review the next summary. Continue the process for about 10 minutes, and then have students return the papers to their authors. At this point, the students rewrite their summaries, making use of the peer feedback, and then turn them in to you.

Get visual. Visuals help students look at content from a different perspective, which can imbue their learning with additional shades of meaning and deepen their brains' representations of the content. One way to go about this is to introduce content using images—simple symbols and stick figures will do. For example, a part of speech could be represented by its function: you could depict an adjective as a blank space in parentheses before a noun, and a verb as a figure angled in motion, with speed lines drawn behind it. Next, let students discuss with partners what they think are the key things to know about the content they have just learned. Then ask students to draw something that represents their learning, ideally within a short time frame of a minute or two. Otherwise, the students may get too bogged down in worrying about the artistic quality of their drawings instead of focusing on the substance.

As an alternative, show the students a template for organizing the content first, before you start teaching. Introduce a graphic organizer that outlines the key areas using both words and some simple drawings, leaving 25 percent of the organizer blank to pique curiosity. After you teach the lesson, let students work in pairs to figure out what was missing from the original organizer. Then ask them to create a graphic organizer consisting entirely of images to help them visualize and organize the content. Have students circulate their organizers for peer editing to gain a broader perspective. Finally, ask students to form groups and share what they have learned from others.

When relevant, have students create a time line to situate the content in the context of their overall learning. For example, in a history lesson, students can examine the events they've studied as part of a sequence of important moments in history, or visualize the time period they're studying in a larger context of what was happening around the world at that time.

Establish meaning through metaphors. Metaphors help students "piggyback" new learning onto their existing knowledge. Creating these associations enables students to build additional context and meaning. Encourage students to develop simple metaphors or analogies to describe new learning in ways that illustrate their understanding. For example, an elementary student could say, "Kangaroos have a pouch to carry their babies, just like my mom has a baby sling for my little sister." A secondary biology student could say, "In the brain, the hippocampus acts like a surge protector because it prevents too much new information from entering the brain." If students are younger, have them choose a metaphor from a list you provide and explain how it connects with a given concept or term.

Tag the text. Text tagging is an engaging process that prompts students to analyze their understanding of content and deepen meaning. Have students go over a previously read or learned section of content and mark it with tags such as checkmarks, exclamation points, and question marks to indicate parts they understood, parts that surprised or intrigued them, and parts that confused them or need more explanation or study. Most digital text formats have a way to mark it. In the paper world, use color-coded sticky tags to identify special features in the text and distinguish different responses you had to the content (e.g., blue = "important," green = "want to know more," and red = "I'm confused"). Then ask students to form teams and share their notes with their peers. Both teaching and learning from fellow students will reinforce their learning.

Build the learning in a model. Like visuals, physical models help students develop a deep, integrated understanding of new learning. In the classroom, creating models could mean anything from constructing a model of the solar system to measuring the rate at which water flows from a faucet to demonstrate Bernoulli's principle, cracking a whip to break the sound barrier, or building a solar-powered oven. A model doesn't have to be a high-tech project; you can make it out of paper, foil, clay, wood, plastic, or almost anything else found in a classroom, kitchen, or office. You can even have students use their bodies as learning models—for example, moving their hands to demonstrate relationships between objects.

Use the power of role-plays. Acting out content or a process reinforces students' understanding and, like visuals and models, allows them to learn about it from a fresh perspective, creating deeper representations of knowledge. In science class, for example, you can have students play atoms and interact with one another to simulate the way some atoms bond to create molecules, and some repel each other. In social studies, students can replicate or reimagine debates between historical figures in government. For example, students can reenact the intense decision-making process that occurred during the Cuban Missile Crisis in 1962. Have students play the roles of President John F. Kennedy, Secretary of Defense Robert McNamara, Attorney General Robert F. Kennedy, and other figures involved in the life-or-death discussion about the best option to save the United States from possible nuclear destruction.

Let students be experts. Giving students the chance to be experts both empowers them to take responsibility for their own learning and increases their retention of the content. One simple activity to try is to give your students new identities: half of the class become experts in the learning topic, and the other half are reporters interviewing the experts. First, divide the class into expert-reporter pairs, and give the reporters two minutes to "get the story"; next, have students reverse roles. Then ask students to debrief the experience with their partners.

Another "expert" strategy is to tell students to turn the content they've learned into a lesson that a 5-year-old could understand, using props and visual aids.

Engage students in in-depth, authentic projects. Nothing puts learning in context more than asking students to apply it to a real-life problem or project. Teaching geometry? Take one week in the middle of the semester and have your class use geometric principles to design a stadium, a golf course, or a racetrack according to specifications you provide. In science, you can have students design solutions to everyday problems, like water contamination or scarce energy resources. In civics class, have students create a model government, including electing a mayor and a city council and setting up a government structure with schools, public works, a parks department, a library, a police department, a fire department, a homeless shelter, and so on.

The teachers who are most successful at getting students on board typically create grand, compelling projects that students care about, and they let students have a voice and make the key decisions. The other key to creating potent, authentic projects is to actually involve some real stakes. The project must have specific, defined criteria; be reviewed by peers; and be designed for or presented before a relevant external audience, such as at a county science fair, a community event, or a city council meeting.

Action #4: Get It Right

In my several decades of teaching, the most humbling realization I've ever had—and that I continue to have—is that the reason learners aren't getting what I'm teaching is not that they're incompetent, but that I'm failing to help them get it right. At the beginning of this chapter, I mentioned that the brain rarely gets new learning right the first time. The reasons are numerous: the teacher could be covering too much content at once, teaching incoherently, or failing to infuse relevancy into either content or instructional style. Or the learner could have low working memory or insufficient background knowledge.

Whatever the reason, it's important not to assume that students understand what you're teaching. Instead, ensure that they are not only learning the content but also retaining it accurately. And make sure to "sell" students on the importance of learning the content accurately by building up their own competencies and confidence and by ensuring that the work you ask them to do is relevant and important. The strategies in the following section will bolster your efforts to help students build more accurate representations of learning.

Solutions You Can Use

Provide a clear, compelling model of what accuracy looks like. Students should know exactly what accuracy looks like for each learning context or assignment. Show your class an example of an accurately completed assignment, checklist, physical model, or illustration. It could be a five-page paper, a website, a multimedia presentation, or a diorama. Explain why the model is accurate, then post it somewhere visible so students can use it as a reference. Next, divide students into pairs or small groups and have them assess a sample assignment or quiz for accuracy, consulting the posted model as needed. After they ascertain whether the sample is, in fact, accurate, question the class to make sure students understand what accuracy for the given assignment looks like.

Support students in creating rubrics. Student-generated rubrics that use a clearly described model of quality and accuracy are a powerful way to help students develop ownership of learning and set out on the path toward accuracy. First, model to your class how to create a rubric, demonstrating the process of developing high-quality success criteria to evaluate the work. Then check for understanding and provide directions and a template for students to create their own rubrics. After students create their rubrics, divide them into pairs or small groups and have them engage in peer editing and error correction. Then guide students in using their completed rubrics and, eventually, have them use the rubrics independently.

Another strategy that also empowers students to assess their own knowledge is to have students pair up and create mini-quizzes with three to five short-answer questions. Have the partners practice on each other at first and then find new partners to test their knowledge.

Engage OPB (other people's brains). Teach students to use "OPB," or outside sources, to check for accuracy and correct errors. Students can practice this process by conducting online fact searches, getting classmates to review and provide feedback on their work, and consulting content experts and relevant texts. Encourage students to make these accuracy checks a habit and ingrain them as an integral step of their work process.

Get students to vote with their feet. Designate different corners or sections of the classroom as potential answers to a multiple-choice question or as positions to take in a debate. Ask the question—for example, "Do you believe the Arab Spring of 2010 and 2011 came about more as a result of internal tensions within the Arab world, or more for international reasons?"—and have students move to the part of the room that best matches their point of view. Ask students in each corner to discuss their thoughts together, and then lead a whole-class discussion. Make sure to follow up with more in-depth questions like "Why did you vote that way?" and "What facts are you basing your answer on?" The question or debate doesn't necessarily have a "right" answer; the point of the activity is to push students to base their responses on an accurate understanding of the facts and to enable the teacher to assess their grasp of the content.

Action #5: Learn to Transfer

The final step of building deep understanding is to help students bring the learning into their own world. Transfer of learning deepens the brain's representations of the content and demonstrates learners' ability to connect the understanding to their own lives or to real-world systems or events. Connecting knowledge across contexts creates a strong representation that is much less likely to be uprooted and forgotten than are discrete facts learned by rote.

Sometimes content experts fail to connect their own in-depth understanding of the subject matter to other areas. In the classroom, this can have dire results. Failing to promote transfer of learning not only results in shallower representations of knowledge but also can lead to student disconnect and apathy. For these reasons, fostering learning transfer is especially crucial for low-SES students, who often lack background knowledge and tend to be more alienated from academic mind-sets than their more affluent peers. Show students how they can turn a passion into a career—for example, a student who writes an essay about justice may go into law enforcement or legal work. Connecting learning to other contexts, including the "real world," will not only deepen students' understanding but also strengthen their sense of empowerment and engagement.

Solutions You Can Use

Make the learning vivid. A great transfer tool is to set learning in the context of your students' world. For example, in an algebra lesson, you could ask, "Would a *Tyrannosaurus rex* be tall enough to be able to stand next to our school and poke its head into the window of our second-story classroom?" Or in physics, ask, "Would a human be able to outrun the poisonous snakes, like you see on TV? How can we figure it out safely?" In a history class, ask, "What events from today will be studied 50 years from now, and why?" or "Will we even have school buildings 50 years from now? If not, why not? If so, how would they be different?" Asking such out-of-the-ordinary questions gives students permission to be creative and come up with fresh ideas. These problems also prompt students to transfer their current knowledge of problem-solving processes to the novel problem at hand.

Infuse questions with real-life detail. Create questions and assignments that drive students to stretch their learning into different contexts. For example, turn a simple math word problem into a finance issue: "If you wanted to turn $10,000 into $1,000,000 in 20 years, what rate of return on your money would you need to make it happen?" Or turn it into a shopping issue: "Which is a better deal: buy three for $10 and get one free, or buy one for $2.55?" Students could turn their insights into visual presentations using PowerPoint, a flip chart, or a tablet.

In social studies and science, ask rigorous, probing questions that test students' ability to develop ideas or beliefs based on their understanding of the content. For example:

- "We are supposed to learn from history. What do you think are the most important lessons for our current president to learn from the last four U.S. presidents? What should he do differently? Write a letter to the president that lists five lessons he should learn from the actions of past presidents."

- "We all know that wasting resources is bad for our planet. But how far are you willing to go to reuse, reduce, and recycle? To what degree would you recycle at home? Would you separate cans, bottles, and newspaper from the rest of the trash? Would you compost garbage? Would you find ways to conserve water? Would you take reusable bags and containers to the store? Would you talk to your neighbors about conserving resources? Would you join a community environmental group? What are your reasons for doing or not doing any of these things?"

Assembling the Puzzle

As we learned in this chapter, pieces of our learning often only gradually come together, as though we're putting together a puzzle. The preceding chapters introduced several core parts of the student-learning puzzle: establishing high expectations, creating a safe class climate, teaching problem-solving skills, and giving students control, among others. This chapter introduced one of the most important puzzle pieces: building profound, enduring understanding.

If you weren't already on board with using engagement strategies to increase academic success, I hope you are after reading this chapter. More than any other, this chapter demonstrates that engagement is not a "soft" strategy: it actually enables students to absorb and retain content, and it is crucial for their success—not just in school but also on whatever paths they take after graduation.

7

Engage for Energy and Focus

The Connecting Engagement Factors

- **Effort and energy:** Energizers help generate the two brain fuels—oxygen and glucose—and increase circulation, and the resulting energy boost leads to positive mind-body states and increased motivation and effort.
- **Mind-set:** Energizers and focusing activities foster positive mind-body states, leading to mind-sets of academic optimism and receptiveness to learning.
- **Cognitive capacity:** Strategies to increase energy and focus boost glucose, dopamine, norepinephrine, and serotonin levels, leading to improved work habits, behavior, and executive function skills.
- **Relationships:** Strategies to increase focus and energy create a positive, fun class climate and forge a strong bond among class members.
- **Stress level:** Strategies to increase energy create positive mind-body states, relieving stress, and strategies to increase focus help students mediate and reduce the effects of stress and provide a sense of empowerment and autonomy.

In the Classroom

Mark is a veteran 9th grade teacher. He loves teaching algebra and is known by some in his school as the "geek of the math department." The first thing you would notice entering his classroom is his passion: he talks excitedly about the subject and encourages students just when they need it. The second thing you would notice is that his students never leave their seats. Perhaps that's the reason afternoon classes are his least favorite. As he says, "The kids just run out of energy. There's nothing left in the tank for them. That makes my job much harder."

Carla, who is only in her second year at the school, also teaches algebra. She is aware of all the negative stereotypes about math being boring. Early in her career, she made a decision: "I promised myself that whatever other flaws I might have, I would never make math dull. I determined to keep kids engaged." Carla devours books and articles about active math and eagerly attends professional development workshops on engagement. Her classes are incredibly active, and, to other teachers' surprise, her students love algebra.

She says, "For me, it all starts with the attitude that I can turn anything into something active. You know how some say students tend to have low energy in the afternoon? That's when my classes become even more active!"

Four Actions to Elevate Energy and Focus

Why do some classrooms just feel electric, buzzing with energy and purpose as students go about their work, while others feel static and dull? In the latter type of classroom, teachers often describe their students as unmotivated or hard to teach. But their real problem is that their classrooms lack both energy and focus.

It may seem surprising to group energy and focus together, but both are crucial to student learning. Energetic students are motivated, awake, and primed for learning. Focused students are able to concentrate on and complete tasks and regulate their work habits and behavior. Together, energy and focus are the twin pillars of an engaging yet academically rigorous environment.

Some teachers may find low-SES students to be especially disconnected or "difficult." As preceding chapters have discussed, disengaged or inappropriate behaviors are often the result of acute or chronic stress and an accompanying sense of powerlessness. We now know that one of the best ways to mitigate these adverse factors is to influence students' mind-body states. You can't always control whether your students ate a nutritious breakfast, but you *can* influence their receptiveness to learning. *All* students, no matter what their socioeconomic status, have trouble managing their own mind-body states; they need your help to have a productive day.

That's where this chapter comes in, laying out four actions that will help you elevate both energy and focus in the classroom. You'll find that you can influence student learning and behavior through exercise and stretches, changes in the environment, and even music.

Four Actions to Elevate Energy and Focus

1. Get students moving.
2. Energize students in their seats.
3. Lower energy to increase focus.
4. Influence energy levels with music.

Action #1: Get Students Moving

Exercise's positive influence on the brain is well established. Physical movement boosts the brain's levels of glucose and key neurotransmitters—including dopamine, norepinephrine, and serotonin—that influence both cognitive and behavioral processes. For example, increased dopamine levels can improve working memory (Söderqvist et al., 2012); norepinephrine boosts focus and memory (Gillberg, Anderzen, Akerstedt, & Sigurdson, 1986); and glucose and serotonin correlate positively with mood, cognitive and behavioral flexibility, and attention (Bequet, Gomez-Merino, Berthelot, & Guezennec, 2001). Exercise enhances executive function (O'Malley, 2011) and semantic memory (Argyropoulos & Muggleton, 2013) and can even help improve the performance of students with reading difficulties (Reynolds, Nicolson, & Hambly, 2003). In addition, a meta-analysis (Reed & Ones, 2006) of 158 studies revealed that brisk aerobic exercise boosts positive emotions, and the effects appear to last for up to 30 minutes post-exercise.

Some secondary schools have reduced or eliminated physical education. That's a big mistake, says Harvard professor Dr. John Ratey. There are strong correlations between physical fitness and academic achievement. In fact, he has documented that engaging in physical activity right before an academic class raises the scores of students in that class (Ratey, 2008). Similarly, for elementary-level students, some of the positive effects of recess have been shown to carry over into academics (Castelli, Hillman, Buck, & Erwin, 2007).

Students don't get such boosts from sitting slumped over their desks all day. Even classroom-based physical activity can enhance cognition and, ultimately, academic achievement (Donnelly & Lambourne, 2011). Teachers get to stand and move most of the day, but students' chairs are no more conducive to learning and engagement than a concrete bus stop. So get students out of their seats now and then to boost blood circulation to the brain and release the stress of bad posture. Even having students stretch or walk around a little keeps them in active metabolic states and primes them to engage in cognitively demanding activities.

A recent surge of research has shown that many childhood games and activities actually aid processing speed, working memory, and attentional skills. Game-based learning has gained credibility as an engaging, effective way to improve learning and retention (Kapp, 2012), and research (Hattie, 2008; Haystead & Marzano, 2009) has found that education programs that include energizing play have a solid 0.46–0.50 effect size when it comes to student achievement.

A fascinating example of the power of play is a study (Wanless et al., 2011) that used the Head-Toes-Knees-Shoulders task to measure self-regulation in 3- to 6-year-old children in four countries: the United States, Taiwan, South Korea, and China. First, the kids in the study learned the original task, and then they were taught to reverse their cues. In this new activity, children were told to perform the response opposite to the one instructed—for example, to touch their heads when told to touch their toes, and vice versa. It seems simple enough, but the researchers found that children who performed well on this task scored higher in literacy, mathematics, and vocabulary than did children who performed less well on the task. The researchers concluded that early behavioral self-regulation is likely important for academic success.

Happily, almost any task can be tweaked to incorporate a self-regulation component. The energizers I describe in the following pages are not just for fun; they also build students' brain power. For example, the "Freeze" activity on page 115 strengthens attention skills and cooperation. If your students are unresponsive, apathetic, or comatose, you need to wake them up by shaking up your own practice. The strategies that follow are easy to implement and will help you infuse energy into a sluggish classroom.

As a general guideline, make sure to use a short energizer at least once every five minutes, and use a longer, more active energizer every half-hour or so. Students have a hard time sitting still for longer than that, and if you don't let them move around periodically, they'll get frustrated, bored, or antsy, and some may start acting out. Each longer energizer should have a purpose and last 2–10 minutes. When finished with the energizer, use a calming, redirecting activity to get students focused on their work again. The following activities are best used to start a class, just after lunch, as transitions, and as brain breaks.

Solutions You Can Use at the Elementary Level

Walk the line. This simple activity builds students' visualization and attention skills. First, create a long, curving line using existing lines on the floor or rug or by using masking or painter's tape. Then have students walk along the line while soft music plays. You can vary this activity by replacing a line with big colored boxes for students to jump onto, floor patterns created with paper shapes, or imaginary obstacles, such as water, grass, broken glass, or snakes.

Freeze. This activity teaches self-regulation and builds students' attention and cooperative skills. Start by playing music while students walk around the classroom. When you stop the music, students must stop walking and quickly get to a nearby "safe zone"—a square marked by an area rug, a mat, or painter's tape. You can make the activity more challenging by removing half of the safe zones so that students must cooperate with one another to find space. You could also use a different color for each zone and, when the music stops, hold up a specific color and have students go to the matching safe zone.

High ten, low ten. This activity builds attention, concentration, self-regulation (i.e., turn taking), and gross motor skills. Have students form pairs and stand facing their partners, about two to three feet apart. Each pair performs a "high ten" by slapping their raised hands (fingertips pointing upward), then a "low ten" by slapping their lowered hands, with the fingertips facing the floor. Play fast music and let students practice for speed. To add variety and complexity, have students add spins, thigh slaps, or handshakes. You could also combine pairs to create foursomes in a square formation, so that each pair must alternate its clapping patterns, keeping an eye on the other pair to avoid their hands colliding.

Follow the directions. Use the basic template of "follow the directions" to create all sorts of variations on the activity that hone students' attention, listening, and gross motor skills. For example, at lower-elementary levels, lead your class in a game of "Barnyard Memory" by calling out the name of a common farm animal (e.g., pig, cow, rooster, horse, or sheep) that students must then mimic, in sound, movement, or both. Then call out a new animal. You could switch it up by letting students call out the animals, or having students repeat all previous animal sounds in addition to each new one.

A variation on this activity is to call out the names of different modes of transportation (e.g., "Bicycle!" "Scooter!" or "Rowboat!"), which students must then pretend to ride, row, pedal, or steer. You could also let students do the callouts, or vary the physical activity: instead of riding a vehicle, have students jump, twist, perform jumping jacks, or play air guitar.

Follow the leader. This activity is similar to the "follow the directions" activities, but it gives students more agency and creates a sense of adventure and a positive social climate. Start by dividing students into groups of three to five and selecting a leader for each group. Each group must follow its leader on a journey that could include walking around the room, jumping, or clapping at will. Once students have mastered the basics, play the slightly more complex and creative "Tour Guide." Each group's tour guide leads his or her followers through imaginary scenarios, such as a jungle, a circulatory system, the solar system, or a zoo. Students must respond to the challenges they encounter by taking appropriate actions, such as ducking, climbing, crawling, or tiptoeing.

Doctor, Doctor. This activity builds students' empathy and cooperation as well as their listening and gross motor skills. First, have students stand up and walk around to music for 10 seconds so that they're in random locations in the classroom. At your signal ("Summer!" "Winter!" "Spring!" or "Fall!"), all students with birthdays in that season must raise their hands and freeze, indicating that they are hurt and need to get to a doctor. It's the job of all the other students in the room to quickly move to the "hurt" students and help them to the nearest chair. You can, of course, use signals other than students' seasons of birth—anything that divides the class into several groups. A variation of this activity is to have the students who raise their hands act as though they have instant memory loss. The other students must provide them with a five-minute update on what's been taught in class that day.

Solutions You Can Use at the Secondary Level

Up and down. If energizers are new to you, start with this simple and safe strategy, which increases blood flow and boosts norepinephrine and dopamine levels to enhance attention and memory. Ask students to stand up, walk to find a partner, and orally review the previous 5 to 10 minutes of the lesson together. You could also have partners do a quick think-pair-share or quiz each other by asking two questions from the current unit. After a couple of minutes, ask students to take their seats again.

Walk and talk. Like the preceding activity, this one increases blood flow and boosts norepinephrine and dopamine levels. Have students pair up and take a four-minute walk around the classroom or outside, if possible, discussing a topic you assign. Inside the classroom, put on upbeat instrumental music to keep them moving. Ask partners to take turns talking, giving notice for them to switch at the two-minute mark. The discussion might center on an essential question like "Why do schools teach mathematics, and does it matter out in the real world?" Discussion topics could also include attitude builders like "GLP" ("What am I *grateful* for? What have I *learned* in the last 24 hours? What is my *promise* for the day?"); Dream and Scheme ("What do you most want to do someday, and what are you doing today to reach that goal?"); or Digging Out of the Dumps ("What's something that has gotten you feeling down in the dumps? How have you dug out of those bad feelings, or how will you in the future?").

Gallery walk critiques. This strategy not only gets students moving and interacting but also builds analytical and observational skills. Have students post their ungraded work (e.g., poems, graphic organizers, outlines, or progress charts) on the walls. While half of the students stand next to their work, the other half walk around to look at everyone's work; then the two groups switch roles. Each student must ask a question about each work and offer one compliment and one suggestion. You can also vary the format—for example, have students form pairs or small teams and display their work at a team table. Half the teams get up and walk around for six minutes to look at the seated teams' work, then the teams switch.

Cross-training simulation. This is another activity that increases blood flow and norepinephrine and dopamine levels. It can also boost motor skills. To start, ask all students to stand. Once they're up, tell them to demonstrate what their body would be doing if they were hitting a baseball with a bat. Then name a new action for a different sport—say, catching a football, shooting a basketball, or rowing crew. Keep moving from sport to sport to give students a cross-training "workout." Eventually, start letting students take turns calling out sports.

Enlist student teams to conduct energizers. Throughout this book, I continually emphasize the importance of having students work in cooperative groups (at the elementary level) or teams (at the secondary level). Cooperative learning builds caring, social skills, and accountability. Getting students to support one another and rely on teammates can make the difference between failure and success. You can further strengthen the social "glue" of your class and create an energetic, collaborative climate by having each team contribute an energizer to the class each week. At first, students may be a bit hesitant, but soon enough a sense of friendly competition will motivate each team to keep coming up with better energizers.

Go on a scavenger hunt. This activity is a good energizer that you can customize for different content areas. Start by asking students to stand up, then ask them to locate and touch, in sequence, five objects in the classroom. Each successive object must be at least 10 feet away from the last one. In math, you could ask students to touch five objects with a right angle, five cylinders, or four cubes. In English, students could touch five items identified with proper nouns and five identified with common nouns. In economics, have students touch five items in order of value or cost.

You can make this a more general energizer by asking students to find five items that begin with the letter *B,* or identify three classmates who share a birth month. You can also ask students to put their own ideas in the class suggestion box, or they could come up with a variation on the activity for their team's weekly energizer.

Ride My Bus. This energizer helps build attention and self-regulation. Plus, it's a *lot* of fun. Begin by selecting a "bus driver," and have that student sit at the front of the class, with the rest of the students sitting behind him or her like passengers. Determine movements that students must make in response to certain actions the driver takes. For example, when the driver leans left, all the passengers lean left—or they lean right. Or when the driver brakes suddenly, all the passengers must jump in their seats—or put up their hands and scream.

Simon Says. This classic game is helpful for developing self-regulation, and you can come up with variations to suit your subject or even a specific lesson. For example, in science, you can say, "Simon says, point to something in this room made of steel. Point to a beaker. Oops, Simon didn't say to do that! Simon says, point to a microscope." In Spanish class, the game is a fun way to practice the language: "Simón dice, toca la boca" ("Simon says, touch your mouth"). Keep in mind, however, that the goal is to have fun and energize the students—*not* to continually trick and embarrass them. Be kind! To vary the activity, let a student lead the activity, or prompt students to do the opposite of whatever "Simon says."

Action #2: Energize Students in Their Seats

In many classrooms, students are pretty sedentary. Some teachers feel unsettled by the prospect of having students moving around the room and would prefer them to stay put. Even in the most dynamic classes, some days it's just not practical to get students moving all around. Although it's not ideal to keep students tethered to their desks during an entire period, there's a lot that can be done even when students stay in their seats. Things as simple as clapping hands or touching acupressure points can increase circulation and energy. Use the following strategies when your classroom needs a jolt of energy but you need students to stay at their desks.

Solutions You Can Use

Simon Says. Divide students into pairs and have partners face each other, either sitting in their chairs or standing in place. One partner takes the role of Simon while the other follows the commands. After a couple of minutes, have partners switch off, so everyone gets a chance to be Simon. You can make this energizer a more challenging memory builder by building on the previous motions. For example, when Simon says, "Simon says, pat your head," the partner begins by following the previous command—say, pointing to the door—before patting his or her head.

Cross-laterals. Cross-lateral movements are an effective brain integration strategy—that is, they require the left and right hemispheres of the brain to work together, which enhances cognition and neuroplasticity. The basic movement is to cross a limb over to the opposite side of the body. For example, have students touch their left hand to their right knee, then their right hand to their left knee, then pat their left shoulder with their right hand, then their right shoulder with their left hand, and so on. Students can also do this in interactive pairs, with partners facing each other and reaching across to slap their right hands together, then their left hands. You can vary the activity by leading students in face and ear cross-laterals. Start by asking students to touch their nose. Then, holding that position, they must cross their free hand over the nose and touch the opposite ear. Then ask them to start again, reversing the movements.

Combine math with movement. At the elementary level, combine a simple math exercise with movement. Pair students up and have them sit in their chairs facing their partners, then start the activity. For example, if students are skip counting, they must touch the floor with their right hand and say, "Two!", then touch the floor with their left hand and say, "Four!" and keep alternating up to the number you name (e.g., 20). You can make the activity more complex for higher grade levels, having students name prime numbers, repeat all previous numbers, or even complete calculations while making physical movements. For example, students could do a cross-lateral shoulder touch, name a number, then do a cross-lateral knee touch and multiply the first number by a new number. A great resource for this type of kinesthetic math activity is Suzy Koontz's Math & Movement program (www.mathandmovement.com).

Trace infinity. This activity improves attention and eye tracking skills, which aid students' abilities to read and focus. Have students face the front of the room. Then ask them to trace the shape of an infinity symbol, starting at the center, with one arm extended in a thumbs-up position. From the center, students' arms go up and to the right, then curve down and back up to the center, then cross over to the other side and repeat, all the while keeping their heads still but following the movement with their eyes. You can vary the activity by reversing the direction or having students use both arms, one after the other, then clasping their hands together into a fist and continuing the movement.

Air swimming. This activity builds students' attention and focus. Have students face the front of the room, standing if possible, and then direct them in air swimming. They can start with a freestyle stroke, rolling one arm forward and then the other. Once they are comfortable with that initial stroke, add some challenge by adding other strokes, such as the breast stroke and the back stroke, or even asking them to do the freestyle stroke with one arm and the back stroke with the other. Once they can do two different strokes simultaneously, have them do the same strokes with the opposite arms.

Use creative handshakes. This activity fosters creativity and strengthens the class's social glue. Ask students to form pairs, face their partners, shake hands, and introduce themselves while making eye contact. Next, ask them to reintroduce themselves with a completely new handshake that they just made up. Students can even integrate other body parts, like their feet or heads.

Write with the body. This activity builds students' focus and memory of key ideas. Start this activity by having students face front. Then choose a couple of key words from the day's lesson and ask students to "write" the words in the air with their fingers. You can vary the activity by asking students to use print or cursive, then switch. Or have students form pairs, with one air-writing while the other tries to read the word. You can also invite students to write with their heads, elbows, knees, or feet, or to air-write the word while announcing its definition aloud. For a more challenging activity, ask students to stand, touching the backs of their chairs for balance. Then tell them to rotate one foot in a circle continuously. Then have them point a finger to a wall, then a window, then a table, and then a neighbor. Finally, while students continue to rotate one foot, have them use the pointing finger to air-write their name.

Come up with team greetings. Team greetings build students' sense of ownership, affiliation, status, and identity. Ask each cooperative group or team in your class to come up with its own name and cheer, and start each class with a high-energy wake-up. Go from group to group, having each one greet the class with its cheer and then choose the next group. A typical cheer might sound like this: [stomp, stomp, clap, clap] "We are group number one, we are here to learn and have fun!" As a variation, have each team leader call out the team name to assemble the team, call attendance within the team, and then report the information to the teacher.

Do the wave. This activity wakes up groggy students and boosts dopamine levels. Divide the room into five different sections, and give each one a distinct label, such as a color. For instance, "Students in this corner are in the blue area." Then explain how the activity works: when you call out a color, the students in that section must stand up and wave their arms slowly from side to side. When you call another color, students in the first section sit down to let the next group stand up and do the wave. Continue until you've called every section, then start again, this time going backward from the last group called to the first group. You could vary the activity by letting students lead and asking them to do something different, like shout out their names.

Rhythm claps. This activity builds listening and attention skills. Start by doing a simple clap that students must repeat. Then make the clapping pattern a little more complicated, adding one or two claps. Keep repeating and varying the process to make it increasingly challenging but still doable. You can switch up the activity by incorporating foot stomps and table thumps or by letting students lead the clapping.

Action #3: Lower Energy to Increase Focus

This section concentrates on narrowing students' focus to either the task at hand or their own thoughts. Focus is an essential skill for students to have in school and in life: it enables them to self-regulate their behavior and enhances cognitive functions such as decision making. In addition, increasing students' focus relieves stress and provides a sense of empowerment and autonomy—both results that are especially powerful for students living in poverty or other adverse circumstances.

Some effective techniques to increase focus include simple and slow stretches or movements, self-talk, mindfulness, and personal reflection. Physical activities, like balancing on low floor objects, stretching, and doing yoga poses, are mentally and physically challenging and drive students to focus closely on the movements. Slow arm movements seem to support creativity and idea generation (Slepian & Ambady, 2012), and simple balancing acts can stimulate brain growth (Taubert, Lohmann, Margulies, Villringer, & Ragert, 2011). When there's a meaningful context to learning, the brain forms connections quickly (Driemeyer, Boyke, Gaser, Büchel, & May, 2008).

For obvious reasons, introspective self-talk is difficult to teach. Nevertheless, studies show that self-talk—positive or negative—has strong effects on behavioral and academic outcomes. Therefore, it's important to explicitly teach students how to replace negative self-talk with positive self-talk. The power of language is surprising in its ability to empower and engage students.

Teaching refocusing and mindfulness, even at the elementary level, has been shown to have lasting benefits (Oberle, Schonert-Reichl, Lawlor, & Thomson, 2012). To learn about building mindfulness, self-regulation, and cognitive function in students, consider consulting the MindUP program (www.thehawnfoundation.org/mindup). Deep breathing and meditation are highly effective in helping students mediate and reduce the effects of stress (Paul, Elam, & Verhulst, 2007). Reflection exercises also help: one study (Ramirez & Beilock, 2011) found that a brief writing assignment in which students expressed their thoughts and worries immediately before taking an important test significantly improved their test scores.

The focusing tasks and techniques in the following section are quiet and simple, but done properly and consistently, they will help you reap powerful rewards.

Solutions You Can Use

Pause and collect. This activity guides students in transitioning from one activity to the next. When students have completed a task or an energizer that took place away from their seats, ask them to return to their desks but remain standing behind their chairs. Then ask them to raise their arms slowly from their sides as they take in a slow, deep breath through the nose. When they have fully raised their arms above their heads, ask students to gently hold their breath for two to five seconds before slowly exhaling through the mouth and lowering their hands to their sides.

Next, tell students to pair up with a neighbor and take turns sharing brief responses to the questions "What are we doing next? What is my goal, and will I reach it?" Once partners have answered the questions, they can have a seat. This brief activity will reorient students both physically and cognitively to what is happening next. Younger students often find the task difficult at first, but they get better with practice.

Mobile mirror. This activity wakes up students and builds their empathy, attention, and focus. Students begin by facing a partner for 20 seconds and trying to mirror each other's movements in slow motion while slow instrumental music plays in the background. At your cue, students must find a new partner. To make the activity more challenging, gradually increase the duration of each round, up to two minutes, and ask students to maintain eye contact the whole time—and no giggling!

Stretch. Ask all students to stand and face the front of the room, and lead them in slow stretches, with fluid arm movements and slow breathing. You can incorporate slow squats, toe points, arm raises, upper-body rotations, shoulder rotations, and leg lifts. Eventually, you can have students lead this activity—first with a neighbor, then in a small group. When they have had plenty of practice, choose a student to lead the whole class.

Balance and point. This activity builds balance and attention skills. Start by asking students to stand. Then ask them to lift one leg and balance on the other. While they balance, give them a task, such as pointing to various places in the room. Then have them switch legs. You can eventually have students balance with one eye closed, then with both eyes closed. Or have students walk on an imaginary balance beam, first forward and then backward. To increase the level of challenge, add a memory component by asking students to recall something from the last week—say, what they had for dinner Tuesday or where they were at 4:30 p.m. on Saturday—while balancing on one leg.

Write to focus. Before an important test, give students a few minutes to stretch their bodies, do some slow breathing, and write about how they feel about the upcoming test. You could give them a prompt if you wish, such as "Will I do well on the upcoming test? How do I know?" As the Ramirez and Beilock (2011) study demonstrated, this seems to calm jitters, especially for habitually anxious students, and improve test results.

Foster positive self-talk. Constructive self-talk is of particular value in motivating goal-directed behavior (Senay, Albarracín, & Noguchi, 2010). Model to students how they can work through an assigned task by telling themselves what they are doing and how they will get it done. Explain what optimism is, why it's important, and how they can generate it: "When you make good, detailed plans and follow through on your goals, you can expect good results." Make sure to teach students proper phrasing, a factor that influences the technique's effectiveness. For example, students do better when they prompt themselves to make a decision rather than use a directive to coerce themselves into action. Give students a list of questions to ask themselves: "Do I have what I need to succeed?" "Do I understand exactly my goal is and what the team goal is?" The question "Will I follow through on my goals?" is much more powerful and more likely to lead to success than the affirmative statement "I will follow through on my goals." Locus of control is a potent factor in students' motivation and decision-making skills. The key is for students to be able to talk in detail about where they are, where they need to be, and what they will be doing to close the gap. You can have students practice the strategy by sharing the self-talk with a partner before using it on themselves.

Enlist student teams to conduct focusing activities. Similar to the strategy on page 118, this activity promotes student teamwork and contributes to a positive class climate. Have each student group or team lead a class focusing activity each week, such as stretching, relaxation, or meditation.

Action #4: Influence Energy Levels with Music

Many teachers already use music in their classroom. It's like having an assistant who helps the day go more smoothly and positively influences your students. The music you play can strongly influence your students' mind-body states and behaviors. Different kinds of music have different effects: music can ramp up norepinephrine, which enhances focusing and memory (Jiang, Scolaro, Bailey, & Chen, 2011); enhance circulation, meaning the brain gets greater blood flow (Trappe, 2010); or release serotonin, which strengthens memory and attention, and dopamine, which supports working memory (Feduccia & Duvauchelle, 2008). Music can mitigate the negative effects of drugs (Tasset et al., 2012) and aid relaxation and ease stress (Jing & Xudong, 2008). The strategies that follow will get you started on using music in powerful ways.

Solutions You Can Use

Know how to choose music. Music works best when it is used purposefully; don't just put on music and then ignore it. Consider the following questions when you plan to incorporate music into a lesson:

- What is the task or activity?
- What is the optimal mind-body state for this activity? Choose carefully: calm? Energized? Silly? Focused?
- Will students need to talk during the task? Never play music with vocals when students need to talk; there will be far too much verbal competition in the brain, resulting in disorganization. Vocalized music is best for high-energy activities, whereas instrumental pieces work better for concentrated, quiet work. Figure 7.1 depicts which music characteristics activate high energy and which lower student energy to increase focus.
- What do your students listen to? Respect the cultures represented in your class: there is always a way to make the classroom feel more a part of your students' world. If you're unfamiliar with their favorite genre, ask for suggestions. Make sure to play nonexplicit versions of any explicit songs.
- Which music selection will likely accomplish your task? If you're not sure exactly where to start, consider consulting the Green Book of Songs

(http://greenbookofsongs.com), which will direct you to songs by subject or theme, organized in such categories as poverty, low self-esteem, children and violence (including bullying), prejudice, and divorce. You'll also find songs related to feelings, such as anger, optimism, motivation, and faith and hope.

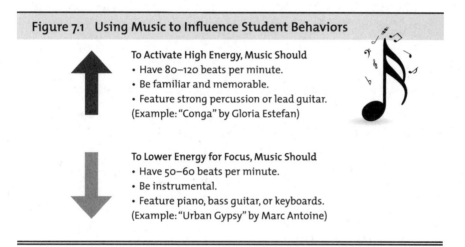

Figure 7.1   Using Music to Influence Student Behaviors

To Activate High Energy, Music Should
• Have 80–120 beats per minute.
• Be familiar and memorable.
• Feature strong percussion or lead guitar.
(Example: "Conga" by Gloria Estefan)

To Lower Energy for Focus, Music Should
• Have 50–60 beats per minute.
• Be instrumental.
• Feature piano, bass guitar, or keyboards.
(Example: "Urban Gypsy" by Marc Antoine)

Answering these questions takes a bit of practice at first, but the process will become automatic over time. You'll be able to run through the list, analyze your lesson's needs, and choose an appropriate song in less than a minute. Learning to maximize the use of music in the classroom is an ongoing process, but when you take a little time to prepare, it can be a powerful contributor to a positive climate. The following list includes various classroom functions and routines that call for certain types of music:

• For seatwork or team discussions: baroque music (e.g., Bach or Vivaldi), smooth jazz, New Age music, or environmental music (e.g., waterfall or ocean sounds)

• For high-energy tasks: classic rhythm and blues, upbeat pop vocals, fast instrumental music, upbeat Latin music (either vocalized or instrumental), classic rock, malt-shop oldies, or punk rock

• For slow focusing activities, such as stretching: instrumental music

- To prompt students to return to their seats (callbacks): songs with a "returning" theme (e.g., "The Heat Is On" by Glenn Frey, "Right Back Where We Started From" by Maxine Nightingale, or "Working My Way Back to You" by the Four Seasons)

- To send students out the door: songs with an uplifting or farewell theme (e.g., "Be the Miracle" by Room For Two, "School's Out" by Alice Cooper, "Enjoy Yourself" by the Jacksons, or "Closing Time" by Semisonic)

- To underline a specific theme, topic, situation, or emotion: country, folk, reggae, contemporary rhythm and blues, or hip-hop

- For group or team presentations or whole-class fun and bonding: sing-alongs from TV show themes and musical theater

- Theme songs for the class: TV show themes

For music to activate high energy, pick from any of the following songs and artists:

- "Zip-a-Dee-Doo-Dah" from *The Disney Collection* CD set
- "Follow the Leader" by the Soca Boys
- "Are You Ready (to Soca Jam)" by the Soca Boys
- "Always Look on the Bright Side of Life" by Costa Crew
- "Life Is Good" by Kenny Chesney
- "The Future's So Bright, I Gotta Wear Shades" by Timbuk 3
- "Positive Vibration" by Bob Marley & the Wailers
- "Rise Up" by R. Kelly
- "Over the Rainbow" by Israel Kamakawiwo'ole
- "That'd Be Alright" by Alan Jackson
- "Walking on Sunshine" by Katrina & the Waves
- "Life Is Good" by Jo Dee Messina
- "Three Little Birds" by Bob Marley & the Wailers

For music to lower energy for focus, try these calming, focusing songs:

- "Positive Thinking" by Acoustic Alchemy
- "Sunset" by Kevoz
- "Country Idyll" by Mason Williams
- "Eye of the Beholder" by Jonn Serrie
- "Goodnight Moon" by Acoustic Eidolon
- "Indian Summer" by David Darling
- "Kari" by Bob James
- "Lullaby of the Ribbons" by Daniel Kobialka

Know how to get and use music. You can purchase MP3s of music from any fee-based platform, such as iTunes. First, though, check out sites that offer free and legal downloads or streaming music, including Amazon, last.fm, or Spotify. You can create playlists in platforms like iTunes or Spotify for different classroom needs or functions, and keep adding to or tweaking them over time. A great resource for finding music by mood is www.allmusic.com/moods. When you click on a mood from the list, like "calm/peaceful" or "lively," the website generates a list of representative albums and songs.

If you need a little help sourcing suitable music, I have two CDs available on Amazon: *Ultimate Music Variety CD,* which includes a wide range of songs that help elevate energy, focus, or calm; and *Greatest Energizer Tunes Ever!,* which includes up-tempo, energizing songs.

To maximize your use of music, here are a few considerations. First, something is better than nothing. Don't wait to use music because you're constantly searching for that perfect piece. The songs you pick don't have to be perfect fits for their accompanying tasks; feel free to experiment and continually explore new options. When you use music in the classroom, you are more important than the actual songs because *you* are the one who sells the idea of the song. So get students' buy-in and charge ahead! Teacher enthusiasm wins over all.

Finally, if you feel too busy and stressed to actually plan, set up, and use music in your class, then you're doing too much talking. Give students an activity to work on individually, with partners, or in teams, and use that time to source and cue up a suitable song for the next transition or activity. There is always time for music.

Making Your Job Better

Even if you don't realize it, you influence your students' mind-body states every day. Your words and actions affect how students think, feel, and behave. The content you teach affects students' states much less than the environment you create. This chapter's techniques for elevating energy and focus aren't just for fun; they are essential parts of your toolbox. They create positive mental and physical states that prime students for learning—and for actually enjoying their time in your classroom.

If you don't like the energy levels you're seeing in your classroom, change what you're doing. Don't explain away the problem with excuses like "It's afternoon, so of course my class is sleepy," or "All these kids eat is junk food; no wonder they're sluggish!" This chapter provides strategies that I have learned through many years of painstaking practice. I know how to keep kids and adults alike engaged all day, and sometimes in the evening. You can do it, too. So take on the challenge! Start believing in yourself, roll up your sleeves, and jump in.

The initial process of reading and managing students' states may consume much of your attention, but over time, this process will become automatic. You will be able to read and influence student states on an unconscious level, and the automaticity of the process will open up more time to focus on other areas that require attention. So stay with it. Although it may seem like a lot of work, in the long run it will make your job easier and more enjoyable. And the rewards are immeasurable.

8

How to Automate Engagement

In the Classroom

David's high school geometry classroom seemed frozen in time; the scene could have been from 50 years ago. His students were mostly quiet. A few were listening to his lecture, but most were spacing out. David's main engagement strategy consisted of calling on those who raised their hands the most. As a result, a select few students talked in class four or five times a day while their classmates never participated.

Down the hall, Judy's classroom, at first glance, looked like pandemonium unleashed. In reality, Judy had carefully constructed and continued to foster a climate of interaction, questioning, and engagement. For a few minutes, students stood working in pairs. Then they returned to their seats to join their home teams. After a team task, Judy led a whole-group activity and then asked students to summarize what they had learned in a solo writing assignment. Some may have found the environment a bit chaotic, but Judy preferred to focus more on learning than on management and compliance.

Later that day, Judy ran into David in the lunchroom. "How's it going?" she asked. David nonchalantly responded, "It's all right, I guess . . . same ol', same ol'." Judy had had this conversation with him before. This time, she decided to try a different tack. "I was wondering if you'd like to check out my class sometime. We definitely do not have the 'same ol', same ol'.' Maybe I could arrange something with the principal, so that you could visit and then we could talk a bit."

David was hesitant. He knew what Judy was doing, but he preferred order to chaos. He told her, "I just think we have different teaching styles. I like to know *what* is going to happen and *when*." Judy assured him, "You know, you can have it both ways: have plenty of engagement *and* predictability. And it even takes less work." David was intrigued.

Five Actions to Automate Engagement

In the preceding vignette, Judy promised David that he could have the best of both worlds: order *and* engagement. Believe it or not, this is possible. Automating engagement means making engagement a routine part of each day. The strategies in this chapter will help you weave engagement into the fabric of your class so that after a while, you won't have to make much extra effort to engage students.

Learning about a good practice, finding a strategy, and using that strategy in the classroom requires initiative, momentum, and effort. Continuing to incorporate the strategy, evaluating results, and making any necessary tweaks requires even more effort, and the process never really ends. It's easy to see how teachers burn out or fall back on old habits.

Automating engagement will make your job easier. It will help you make better use of your limited instructional time, ensure students are continually engaged, and reduce stress. These tools also empower students to take greater ownership of their learning. All students, especially those living in poverty or other adverse circumstances, crave relevant tasks and a sense of control. When students own their learning, they begin to engage on their own. When they engage on their own, their progress goes into overdrive.

The need for automation is simple. There is enough to worry about without needing to solve every single problem each day. Automation requires a bit more energy up front to get the payoff later on, but consider it an investment toward an enhanced quality of life. The five actions laid out in this chapter will show you how to automate engagement in your own class or school.

Five Actions to Automate Engagement

1. Establish rituals.
2. Foster leadership and teamwork.
3. Captivate with curriculum.
4. Integrate technology.
5. Cultivate schoolwide social support.

Action #1: Establish Rituals

Throughout life, we all use social rituals like weddings and funerals to mark certain milestones, and we tend to follow a set of cultural rules about how each of these events unfolds. These rules are important: they strengthen our social tissue and convey values and a sense of order to ourselves and to younger generations (Krause, 2011). When children attend a wedding, even when they misbehave, they get a glimpse into their future. They see the start of a couple's lifelong union and learn the value that society places on that union.

Rituals also have a powerful place in the classroom. Even simple rituals can enable you to meet daily needs and resolve problems in ways that add energy to your classroom. This last point is key: rituals aren't meant to be just one more chore on your to-do list; done well, they lighten existing burdens. They establish classwide responses to recurring classroom needs, including starting class on time, taking attendance, making announcements, getting the class's attention, dealing with visitors and interruptions, distributing supplies, collecting assignments or materials from students, leading energizers or stretch breaks, celebrating student successes or birthdays, cleaning up work areas, and closing the class. Rituals can help you address all of these while increasing student engagement and making life generally easier.

For many reasons, rituals are especially important for low-SES students and other students living in adverse circumstances. They provide a sense of community and stability, which helps lower stress levels, and they enable issues to be addressed in productive, student-centered ways. Rituals have a positive influence on student behavior because they help teachers manage students' mind-body states and elevate student engagement and productivity. They provide a sense of well-being and strengthen the social glue that binds every class.

It is important to distinguish rituals from procedures and routines. Whereas a *procedure* is any predictable action (e.g., taking attendance), and a *routine* is a series of procedures strung together (e.g., the steps you take to begin your class each day), a *ritual* is a regularly repeated, orchestrated event that meets a recurring need (e.g., a celebration of success). Procedures and routines are useful tools, but rituals go further (see Figure 8.1).

The five criteria listed in Figure 8.1 highlight that the ritual is not about the teacher alone; it must engage a *collective effort* to meet a *group need*. If you blow a train whistle to get students' attention, you're not actively engaging students to address the issue you're trying to resolve; in fact, you're making more work for yourself. The train whistle is *your* ritual, not theirs. It's missing the crucial component that draws students in emotionally, so even if they do respond initially, they will quickly lose interest, and the ritual will fail to get the desired effect.

To make the train whistle procedure a true ritual, you could tell your class, "Students, when I have a really important idea, I want to know if you're ready for it. When I blow my train whistle, you respond with 'All aboard!'

Figure 8.1 What Makes Rituals Effective?

Highly effective classroom rituals

1. Address a real, recurring need. (Students need to see the relevancy.)

2. Include and engage everyone, every time, at the same pace. (To get classwide participation, all students must feel included.)

3. Are simple and easy to perform. (Students must be able to perform the ritual automatically.)

4. Are predictable. (Students should be ready for it every time.)

5. End with students in a positive emotional state. (Students need an emotional reward to repeat the ritual.)

Rituals Allow You to Press "Play"

Now, let's try it out." *That* is a ritual: it addresses a need, it engages everyone, it's simple, it puts everyone in the same state of anticipation, and it builds community as everyone responds to the prompt in unison. By enlisting students' help in this way, you grant them a level of ownership over their learning while helping class run more smoothly.

To get started on using rituals in your classroom, follow these three steps:

1. Pick a problem to solve or a need to address.

2. Design a ritual that meets the five criteria (or use one provided here), and set a day and time to try it out.

3. Debrief how the ritual went, and tweak it as needed.

When you introduce your class to the new ritual, what matter most are your enthusiasm and consistency. You don't have to be perfect at it; just do it! Be confident about the ritual; assume it will work, and your students will be more likely to buy into it. Revise the ritual as necessary and repeat until it's automated. Then you can add a second ritual to meet a different need. Keep up the cycle of introducing, reviewing, and revising rituals until they're automated and adding new ones.

Once rituals become automated, students will remember them even if you forget. Often, students will remind the teacher to start or complete a ritual. That's when you know the rituals are working! One caveat is that over time, students will tire of any ritual; they tend to get desensitized to repeated events as the novelty wears off. So make sure to change each ritual slightly every month or so (at the secondary level) or every six to eight weeks (at the elementary level), or whenever you sense students disengaging.

You can tweak the current ritual or establish a new one. This isn't as daunting as it sounds; you don't need to create 10 rituals for each classroom need for the year. Instead, you could come up with three or four rituals for one classroom need, such as attendance, and rotate them monthly. Students can get "re-sensitized" to a familiar ritual when they haven't used it in a few months. You can even let students come up with a ritual; consider holding a class contest and inviting students to invent a new ritual as an individual or a team project. Just make sure that it meets the five key criteria of powerful classroom rituals listed in Figure 8.1

The following strategies will guide you in developing rituals to address various classroom needs.

Solutions You Can Use

Start class with a ritual. This is perhaps the most important item on the list of classroom needs to address. Class needs to start on time and in a positive manner every single day, for weeks and months on end. Here is an example of a highly effective ritual.

- *Ritual name:* Welcome Back

- *When the ritual is used:* At the beginning of every class, as students enter the classroom

- *How it works:* Play your designated callback song as a trigger to bring students back to their seats and signal them to be ready to learn. The song should be positive and energetic. At the elementary level, some good callback songs include "One Thing" by One Direction, "No Worries" by Simon Webbe, and "Walking on Sunshine" by Katrina and the Waves. At the secondary level, play a song like "Are You Ready (to Soca Jam)" by the Soca Boys, "Stay Positive" by Cali P., or "Livin' la Vida Loca" by Ricky Martin.

Students know they must reach their seats before the song is over. The second the song ends, say, "If you made it back on time, please raise your hand and say, 'Yes!'" Model the behavior by raising your own hand and saying, "Yes!" Then tell students to give their neighbors the appropriate greeting. If it's the first period, or the only period this group meets during that day, tell students, "Now turn to your neighbor and say, 'Happy Monday to you!'" If students have returned from recess or lunch, tell students, "Now turn to your neighbor and say, 'Welcome back!'" Students follow the cues. Afterward, the classroom is quiet for a moment, and anticipation is high.

• *Result:* The class starts on an organized yet positive note, with everyone in a state that is receptive to learning. During that brief moment of quiet after students follow the cues, the class is in a state of anticipation. That's when you jump in and begin class.

Notice that students who were talking are not admonished to be quiet; they are simply asked to say a single positive word: "yes." This is smart because it's easier to get chatty students to say "Yes!" than it is to get them to be quiet. Students are then asked to recognize that they are in a social environment and to acknowledge a neighbor with an affirmation.

Here's another ritual you can use to start class. It's a simple call-and-response procedure that can work for any subject area.

Teacher: "Who's here?"
Students: "We're here." [Students point to a neighbor.]
Teacher: "To do what?"
Students: "To learn and grow!" [Students point to their heads.]
Teacher: "How will we do it?"
Students: "Work hard and be our best." [Students hold out their arms.]
Teacher: "When do we start?"
Students: "Right now, with zest!" [Students pound their desks.]

The couple of seconds of silence that follow these opening rituals are your cue to jump in and start class. If you wait too long, it will get noisy again.

Note that both of these rituals fit the five criteria listed in Figure 8.1. Their beauty is that they meet a recurring need in an elegant way. There's no need to shush or berate students, give them the evil eye, or raise your voice. The rituals are short, precise, and fun.

Get the class's attention. Like the last strategy, this one addresses a fundamental need in any classroom: getting your students' attention. You can use this strategy at almost any hour of the day, or at any point in a class period, but use it *in addition* to the start-up ritual, not instead of it; the two rituals shouldn't be mixed up.

- *Ritual name:* Whoosh!

- *When the ritual is used:* At the beginning of an activity that requires the class's full attention

- *How it works:* Stand up, make eye contact with the group, and clap loudly three quick times in succession. You can also have a student do this if he or she is leading a team or the class in an activity. When students hear the three claps, they realize someone needs not only their attention but also their support in listening. Students clap three times to show they're ready to pay attention. Then they ball up their hands and throw them forward, as though they're passing an imaginary ball of energy toward you, and say, "Whoosh!" You are now ready to speak.

- *Result:* The class is now in an attentive, listening state.

Contrast this high-energy ritual to the low-energy procedure of asking students to raise their hands to indicate that they're paying attention. The latter procedure fails to elevate energy or focus, give students agency, or build community. Pretty soon, students will raise their hands half-heartedly, and the whole process will seem boring and painful.

Leave on a high note. This ritual ensures that students leave class on a high note every day, with a sense of completion and anticipation for tomorrow.

- *Ritual name:* The "Yes" Clap

- *When the ritual is used:* At the end of the school day (or class, if it's the only period this group meets during the day), to celebrate students' learning

- *How it works:* Have students stand facing you or their teammates, with their hands stretched out from each side, palms up. Say, "Use your imagination to put all of your previous knowledge, whatever you brought with you today, in your left hand. Put all the new material you have learned today in your right hand. When I say so, bring them together in a huge, roaring clap, and shout the most powerful word in the English language: 'Yes!'" After the synchronous clap, students feel energized and ready to leave on a high note. Following the clap, as students exit, play positive, fun music—something hip and upbeat that fits the mood.

- *Result:* Students charge out the door in an energized mode, feeling positive about the class and already receptive to tomorrow's learning.

Celebrate milestones. It's important to celebrate milestones like student birthdays in some way. Celebrating birthdays lets students know that you see them as people, not just students, and that you recognize and care about their lives outside school.

- *Ritual name:* Birthday Bash

- *When the ritual is used:* Each Monday, post and celebrate any birthdays for that week.

- *How it works:* Wait until the opening class ritual is complete, and students are still standing. Then invite the birthday students' teams to lead the ritual by saying, "Hey, we have two birthdays to celebrate this week! Eric's team and Diane's team, come up front. You know what to do!" Each birthday student's group then leads the class in a cheer or celebration of their choice. The entire class ends the ritual with a round of applause.

- *Result:* The birthday students feel recognized and valued, and everyone in the class feels like part of a community. In addition, students feel empowered by leading the cheer themselves.

Deal with interruption. Every teacher must deal with distractions or class visitors now and then. Here is one way to address the issue.

- *Ritual name:* Hail to the Chief

- *When the ritual is used:* Whenever someone visits your class, or during any other outside interruption

- *How it works:* Walk over to the visitor and find out what he or she needs while students stand and wait for you to give a signal. If the visitor needs only a short moment of your time, hold up one finger. This tells students to remain standing and to feel free to stretch or talk with their neighbors until further notice. If the visitor needs more of your time, hold up two fingers. This tells students to have a seat and work on a pre-arranged task listed on the board. When the visitor leaves, the students give him or her a seated or standing ovation.

- *Result:* This ritual makes the best of a potential distraction by giving students a stretch break and either a chance to socialize or a signal to refocus on the task at hand. By acknowledging the visitor instead of telling students to ignore the interruption, you are able to maintain student energy and focus.

Action #2: Foster Leadership and Teamwork

Leadership and teamwork are powerful factors in automating student engagement. Taking leadership roles and collaborating in teams increase student responsibility and help students become more confident. The more self-reliant students become, the more control they feel over their learning, and the more likely they are to actively engage as a matter of routine.

Developing students' leadership skills begins with granting incremental increases in responsibility to students while providing relevant instruction in the skills they need to succeed, offering encouragement, and holding them accountable for the obligations they take on. Show students how to define learning goals and problems in ways that are meaningful and relevant to them. Give them explicit measures and criteria for success to enable them to assess their own progress and make decisions about next steps. Help them understand that the journey to true leadership holds them to a high standard of excellence and doesn't support excuses.

Teaching students to work in teams will also help you automate engagement in your classroom, although it does require some effort and time investment. Before you start, internalize the five key criteria of successful small-group learning, which apply to both elementary-level cooperative groups and secondary-level cooperative teams:

1. **Positive interdependence.** A common factor in the classrooms of teachers who work successfully with kids from poverty is a high level of *interdependence*—that is, all members of the class are mutually dependent on one another. Many students who grow up in adverse circumstances come to school as "survivors" and think of themselves first. Instead of complaining that your kids "don't care," show that *you* care, and then show them how to care about others. In cooperative groups and teams, encourage students to feel responsible for both their own effort and the whole group's effort. Interdependence is a key part of what automates the class's daily academic and social "work."

2. **Individual and group accountability.** Each student is responsible for doing his or her part, and the group is accountable for meeting its collective goal.

3. **Face-to-face interaction.** Making actual eye contact with fellow group members encourages support, discussion, and accountability.

4. **Group processing.** Students understand, analyze, and debrief both their own and the group's capacity to work successfully.

5. **Group behaviors.** Students receive clear instruction in the social skills needed to succeed together, and they use those skills in their group work. (Johnson & Johnson, 1999)

The roles you choose for cooperative groups and teams must in some way fulfill these five criteria. Some sample roles for elementary-level cooperative groups include the following:

• The **group leader** could be the organizer, communicating to the group the overall structure of a project's process, or the spokesperson, who presents the group's work to the rest of the class. The leader is ultimately responsible for the group's success.

• The **secretary** records important information, such as directions or expectations for each group member.

- The **assistant teacher** makes sure that all group members understand the concepts and the group's conclusions, moderates discussions, and ensures that everyone has fulfilled his or her role. The student in this role also summarizes the group's conclusions and evaluates the progress of each session.
- The **encourager** provides emotional support, acts as the team cheerleader, and models and reinforces appropriate social skills and behaviors.
- The **logistics manager** takes care of supplies and timekeeping, keeping the group on task and ensuring it has the materials it needs, and is the liaison between group and teacher.

Some sample roles for secondary-level cooperative teams include the following:

- The **CEO** runs the team's work, keeps everyone on task, and manages time.
- The **HR representative** fosters positive, productive social interaction and oversees team ethics and job performance.
- The **PR spokesperson** is in charge of interactions with other teams and manages public communications, such as presentations and Twitter updates.
- The **tech and logistics manager** makes audio recordings of team meetings, uses software to create and update team documents, and procures needed supplies.
- The **team temp** has no fixed role but is "in training," learning from others how to perform their roles and taking over for absent team members when necessary.

At all levels, make sure to have students engage in team building by selecting a leader, choosing a special place to sit, and coming up with a team name, cheer, and logo. Teams can also create a unique celebration cheer to use when they complete a task or reach a milestone and a rubric to assess their work on the project or unit. Roles within cooperative groups or teams should rotate so that everyone gets a chance to do every role.

Solutions You Can Use

Teach students a simple leadership model. The following model helps students internalize leadership skills, hold themselves accountable for their progress, and make changes to their strategy as needed.

1. Teach students how to self-evaluate. Give students a series of simple questions to help them understand themselves better. The questions could include

   - What are my strongest academic skills (e.g., attention, studying, or memory)?

   - What are my best qualities or traits (e.g., honesty, caring, fairness, or positivity)?

   - What do I need to get better at to improve my grades (e.g., study skills, reading, or math)?

   - How will I improve (e.g., ask for help from the teacher, a team member, or a parent)?

   - What are my goals for the next month (e.g., improved test performance, better grades, or stronger friendships)?

2. Teach planning and goal setting. Many teachers assume that students have already learned study skills from previous teachers and that any failure to study is an effort or attitude problem. Actually, it's often a strategy problem. Teach students how to focus on habitual study periods in a regular study area and set realistic goals.

3. Help with strategy implementation. Help students prioritize and select learning, study, and project strategies and develop contingency plans in case the selected strategy doesn't work.

4. Support students' outcome monitoring and strategy correction. Teach students how to troubleshoot problems, brainstorm hypotheses about what might not be working, and make a list of plausible choices of a new strategy. Teach them how to evaluate the choices, pick the criteria for the choices, and make the changes.

Foster leadership at the elementary level. At the K–5 level, you can introduce leadership to students by having them form cooperative groups that include a leader and three other roles. Assigning each group member a different role begins students' process of understanding what leaders do.

Another way to promote leadership and make students feel like part of the class community is to invite their input. For example, you can pick a couple of students to hold up signs reading "Stretch break" or "Need new tunes" at the appropriate points in a lesson. Keep in mind that you're not obligated to follow all of your students' directions, only to appreciate their input and consider their point of view. In addition, consider keeping a suggestion box in the classroom. Read aloud a few suggestions each week, and every now and then accept one of the suggestions.

Once you're ready to start building up students' attitudes and aspirations for leadership, have them start treating their classroom jobs more seriously. But before you expect students to take their jobs seriously, *you* need to take them seriously, too. Many job titles in the elementary classroom are, if not entirely meaningless, the epitome of low expectations: a pencil sharpener, a light monitor, a caboose. Have you ever had a student tell you, "I want to be a line leader when I grow up!"? So upgrade every single one of these existing job titles so that it reflects its closest real-world equivalent. The line leader becomes the tour guide, the light monitor becomes the electrician, the caboose becomes the security guard, the messenger becomes the FedEx agent, and the stretch leader becomes the fitness instructor. The jobs remain the same, but the way students *think* about them changes. When you work with students from poverty, it's particularly important to set goals and dreams in an authentic context.

Foster leadership at the secondary level. At the secondary level, add two ranks to the class job structure: associates and leaders. Every student starts as an associate. Examples of associate jobs include logistics manager, who keeps track of class supplies, and energy manager, who signals the teacher for team-led stretch breaks and energizers. Leader jobs would include class DJ, who selects and plays the music in class, and fitness or dance instructor, who leads class stretches and energizers.

To get an associate job, students need to complete a résumé, which helps develop concise writing skills, and an interview, which helps develop speaking skills. The application process as a whole builds critical thinking skills. Once a student has been an associate for 30 days, he or she can apply to be a leader, again submitting a résumé and undergoing an interview. After getting a leader job, students will be subject to progress reviews to hold them accountable for their work.

Get students involved in the community. A powerful way to build leadership and teamwork is to get students involved in their community. You can engage them in school volunteer projects, like building or grounds beautification, tutoring, or mentoring, or encourage them to visit Volunteer Match (www.volunteermatch.org) or Youth Service America (www.ysa.org) to find outside volunteer opportunities.

In addition, get them interested in business and entrepreneurship. Biz-World (www.bizworld.org), for example, is a project-based program that has intermediate-level students run a business in a simulated industry.

Finally, encourage leadership by connecting students with youth leadership programs. Check out the National Honor Society's online list of national youth leadership organizations (www.nhs.us/Content.aspx?topic=28339) and encourage students to seek out a local chapter. In addition, the Global Youth Leadership Summit is a powerful program that builds students' leadership skills. Even if your students aren't able to attend the annual summit, you can show them YouTube clips of the speakers for inspiration (www.youtube.com/watch?v=qSOFXtk28oA).

Let teams take over. Student groups and teams should be automating many everyday classroom routines. Teams are a useful tool for you to use to increase and automate engagement, so use them! For example, have teams take their own attendance and turn in their tally to you. If everyone in a team is present, the team celebrates. A team also celebrates after it leads an activity or succeeds on a project. These empowering team tasks and celebrations build community and encourage active participation.

You can also enlist teams to help you manage mind-body states in the classroom. To get all students in a positive, energized state that is receptive to learning, say, "Everyone point to your team leader." Then add, "Team leaders, you have 60 seconds to decide on what activity your team will lead next week, whether it's a stretch or an energizer. Team members, turn to your team leader and say, 'Let's do it!'" Make sure to follow through by having each team lead a weekly calming stretch or high-energy activity. Give teams bonus points for providing sneak previews of "coming attractions" (e.g., upcoming class content or school events) or memory joggers of anything the class learned in the last week. Sneak previews and memory joggers should last less than a minute.

Action #3: Captivate with Curriculum

One of the best ways to automate engagement in the classroom is simply to make class so interesting that students *want* to engage. This action invites you to locate, develop, and embed curriculum that, by its design, engages students.

Traditional curriculum that relies heavily on textbooks and a lecture format and moves learning at a district-mandated pace is just setting students up for boredom. The key to engaging students with curriculum is to tie it to real life. Connect, connect, and connect some more. Every high-performing teacher I've studied makes profound, authentic connections between the content and their students' own lives.

Students, especially low-SES students, need a sense of relevance to fully engage. Focus more units around longer-term projects that require students to work with partners or in teams, conduct research on real-life issues, write up findings, present the material to the class, and even extend their learning by putting their results into action. Provide enough variety that students look forward to every day as a new opportunity to learn. Project-based learning in particular almost guarantees increased engagement, and high-quality career and technical education can support student interests while dramatically increasing high school graduation rates (Kulik, 1998).

Solutions You Can Use

Incorporate issues that connect. Project-based learning is one of the best ways to integrate real-world issues and authentic tasks into your curriculum. Assigning projects that drive students to learn about and tackle real-life issues gives students an authentic context in which to apply their learned skills and helps them see the big picture of life beyond school and their current situations. They get a real sense of self-efficacy and feel motivated to learn because they know they're working toward something bigger.

Award-winning teacher Katie Lyons, who teaches social studies in a low-income Chicago school, engages students by connecting history to their own lives and setting it in the context of the rich, diverse neighborhood around them. For an inquiry-based historical research project, she brought students to the Chicago History Museum to let them explore and identify personally resonant, meaningful topics. She gave them a choice in the medium of their final project: they could develop and communicate their learning through a website, an exhibit, a paper, a documentary, or a performance. She set the bar high and created an authentic goal: students were required to present their research projects publicly, to an audience of peers and judges at the school's history fair. The student-created websites and documentaries were available to anyone with Internet access.

If you're new to this approach, consult the *Educational Leadership* article "Seven Essentials for Project-Based Learning" (Larmer & Mergendoller, 2010), and visit www.edutopia.org/project-based-learning for helpful advice and examples of how actual teachers are using project-based learning in the classroom.

Embed real-life professions and trades in the curriculum. Another great way to infuse relevance in the existing curriculum is to repurpose it so that it teaches students about real-life issues and industries while still address-ing the standards. Be creative: you might be surprised by how many subject areas relate to a given field or industry. You'll engage students with a wider range of authentic curriculum including (but not limited to) traditional courses. For example, help your secondary-level students become more job-ready by teaching a unit on entrepreneurship. Kids love the idea of learning how to start a business. In an English language arts class, teach students how to write a proposal or a business plan and develop their writing skills in PR and marketing. In a math class, teach students how to add up sales, predict and manage the supply chain, create and analyze spreadsheets, and gener-ate profit-and-loss statements. A semester-long math course can be taught through the eyes of a businessperson.

The following list includes various ideas for units based on real-life industries or professions and a few sample topics or subjects that relate to each profession. As you can see, whatever content area you teach, you should be able to find a way to connect an authentic professional field or trade to your curriculum.

- A unit on animal and food science could incorporate agriculture, nutrition, environmental studies, animal husbandry, or veterinary science. Relevant subject areas include ecology, environmental science, health, economics, political science, and agricultural studies.

- A unit on the arts could incorporate dance, calligraphy, acting, music, animation, painting, literature, or theater marketing. Relevant subject areas include art, music, theater, English, marketing, and computer science.

- A unit on automobiles could incorporate body repair, auto mechanics, small engine repair, driver education, or green vehicles and fuels. Relevant subject areas include automotive studies, physics, engineering, environmental science, and political science.

- A unit on the building trades could incorporate industrial arts, technical drawing, architecture, carpentry and woodworking, construction, electrical wiring, plumbing, or interior design. Relevant subject areas include wood shop, math, science, engineering, vocational education classes, and art.

- A unit on business management or entrepreneurship could incorporate finance, accounting, marketing, graphic communications, multimedia production, principles of business, social media, or web design. Relevant subject areas include English, math, accounting, business administration, marketing, art, and computer science.

- A unit on computers could incorporate software design, graphic design, information literacy, programming, game design, or robotics. Relevant subject areas include English, art, math, physics, and computer science.

- A unit on film could incorporate cinematography, audio production, set design, set construction, film history, music, or animation. Relevant subject areas include English, art, history, music, wood shop, computer science, and vocational education classes.

• A unit on hospitality could incorporate culinary arts, hotel management, horticulture, event planning, or marketing. Relevant subject areas include vocational education classes, family and consumer sciences, English, and marketing.

Have students run a mini-city. Like the Classroom City program in Chapter 5 (p. 75), this strategy has students take on all the roles in a small city as a way of creating relevance and community and developing students' responsibility and initiative. You can walk students through the job application process and teach them important job skills like time management, professional behavior, interviewing skills, and so on. Every day, students do the work that runs the city.

Action #4: Integrate Technology

Incorporating technology in your classroom blends the fast-moving changes in the world with curriculum in ways that invite and even compel students to actively engage. Students are already fascinated by technology in their daily lives, so it's not a stretch to see how using technology can help automate student engagement. In addition, teaching with technology can build valuable 21st century skills that students will need in higher education or the workplace. Using technology in the classroom also helps level the playing field for low-SES students, who are less likely than their higher-SES peers to have their own computers or Internet access at home.

Keep in mind, however, that buying an iPad for every student won't guarantee a single percentage point increase in student achievement. Low achievement scores are a people problem and need people-driven solutions. It is therefore vital to use technology strategically and purposefully, as both an engagement tool *and* a learning tool. Just playing random computer games won't help anyone. Be thoughtful about the integration of technology, include students, and remember that it is a means to an end, not an end in itself. The strategies that follow discuss ways you can use technology to promote students' acquisition of knowledge, to enable students to demonstrate and share learning, and to assess students' learning.

Solutions You Can Use

Use technology to promote knowledge and skill acquisition. Technology can be a huge boon in helping students access and retain knowledge and skills. Desktop, laptop, and tablet computers and Internet access can open up a world of knowledge and research capabilities in the classroom. In schools that can't afford to buy enough devices for all students to use regularly, teachers and administrators can write grants to build technological capacity.

One high-poverty high school in North Long Beach, California, never has issues with engagement. Marvin Smith, the cofounder of Doris Topsy-Elvord Academy (DTEA), has developed a school that provides vital opportunities for low-income students. DTEA, which has a rigorous academic preparation and college readiness curriculum, focuses on purposeful engagement through technology. Students apply technological solutions such as multimedia presentation software, spreadsheet applications, web design tools, project management tools, and computer-aided design to both academic and real-world contexts. They make use of technology and explicitly taught leadership skills to engage in entrepreneurship projects, designing and implementing micro-enterprises. Graduation rates are through the roof, and students love coming to school.

In addition, research-based software programs can serve as effective complements to instruction in various subject areas. Scientific Learning, for example, provides several products to assist students in reading comprehension, including Fast ForWord and Reading Assistant. These programs engage students with game-like formats, but their exercises are quite challenging and effective, increasing neuroplasticity through strategic use of novelty, challenge, and activity duration and providing individualized support and feedback. As mentioned in Chapter 4, websites like www.junglememory.com and www.lumosity.com can help build students' attention skills and working memory.

Use technology to demonstrate and share learning. Many software and hardware tools enable students to share their learning with others more easily and effectively than was possible even in the recent past. For example, you can now have students store and share files in the cloud rather than on a hard drive, which opens up new potential for collaboration with and feedback from peers as well as you. You can also have students use handheld pico projectors to conduct presentations for their teams or the whole class. These projectors, about the size of a deck of cards, remove the need for clunky, expensive audiovisual equipment. They not only store content but also have built-in projectors that enable users to clearly project images anywhere—on a wall, a table, or even a clipboard. An increasing number of devices with the potential to demonstrate and disseminate learning are being developed all the time: your school may soon have its own 3D printer and display device. Aside from their obvious wow factor, such devices are impressive in their potential to build cooperative learning skills, awaken students' creativity and vision, and familiarize students with technologies they may need to use in college or the workplace.

Use technology to assess student learning. Technology has made some great strides in the realm of student assessment, especially with the development of classroom response systems (CRS), sometimes known as student or audience response systems. In addition to increasing classroom interaction and engagement, CRS is a powerful formative assessment tool. Here's how it works. A teacher poses a true/false or multiple-choice question to the class via an interactive whiteboard or projector, and students respond using handheld clickers that transmit their answers to the teacher's computer. The computer's software sorts and analyzes students' answers and creates charts or reports indicating how well students learned the content. The teacher can then make real-time adjustments to instruction based on the results, such as leading students in a discussion of the merits of each answer choice or asking students to discuss the question in small groups, and reviewing the content as needed. If a CRS is out of your school's budget, consider having students use their cellphones as response devices (as long as all students have cellphones or are able to share one with a partner) by texting you their answers.

Technology can also enable teachers to assess performance in other areas, such as performing arts or public speaking. For example, you can use a compact digital video camera (or, if that's out of reach, just about any cellphone) to record and instantly view movies of students' dance, drama, or music performances or oral reports for review and critique.

Action #5: Cultivate Schoolwide Social Support

Up to this point, I've been talking about how teachers can automate student engagement, but it is equally important to automate engagement among staff members. Engagement is contagious: students are more likely to feel excited about being at school when their teachers are. Accordingly, this section shifts our focus from the classroom to the school as a whole and describes steps leaders—including teacher leaders and department heads—can take.

The term *priming the pump*, which generally refers to taking some action to stimulate flow or growth, comes from the procedure required to pump water from a dry well: water must be flushed back into the pump to create enough suction and pressure that water can be pumped again. The concept applies across numerous arenas: you prime the pump to get water, to stimulate the economy, and to get active, schoolwide engagement.

In the context of school engagement, priming the pump means creating the conditions in which engagement can flourish. These conditions include a social system that fosters an ongoing flow of ideas, feedback, and support. Within a strong social system, students who are engaged in one class are more likely to carry that energy to other classes, and teachers will more openly share ideas, resulting in greater collaboration and competence all around. The three essential factors that make up a strong social system are staff trust, actionable collaboration, and timely habits of cooperation.

Staff trust is the foundation of the system and a key part of boosting student achievement. Bryk (2010) found that schools with low trust had only a 1 in 7 chance of improving student scores in reading and math, whereas schools with strong climates of trust had a 1 in 2 chance of improvement. Trust building is often overlooked in favor of more obvious, pressing issues, but the absence of trust in a school is all too conspicuous. Schools that lack trust consistently have difficulty in transformation. The book *Fired Up or Burned Out* (Stallard, 2007), which examined the factors that determine whether organizations are disconnected or impassioned, concluded that "emotional" factors were four times more effective in increasing employee engagement and effort than were "rational" factors. The book further explains that "emotional contagion," which emanates from a group of energized, connected colleagues, perpetuates positive connections and effort throughout the institution. When staff members trust one another, they are more likely to collaborate on policies and strategies and on what constitutes strong implementation of those strategies.

Actionable collaboration, the second factor of a strong social system, refers not only to sharing ideas but also to coming up with steps to implement those ideas. In contrast to the typical *teacher* mind-set of change (which focuses on the need for a new classroom strategy) and the typical *leader* mind-set of change (which focuses on the need for a strategy plus solid execution), a successful *change agent* mind-set focuses on the need for data-driven strategies that are well executed, debriefed, and modified in a highly trusting, collaborative environment.

Staff members at high-performing schools ask themselves, "Where are we? Where are we trying to go? What do we need to do to get there?" Notice that these questions leave no room for complaints or excuses. Staff meetings should focus on which strategy to use and when and how to use it. After teachers have used the strategy, they should discuss how it worked and how they can adapt it to meet specific needs. When you lead these meetings, share what has worked for you, and be willing to listen to others' ideas. Create a staff culture of can-do optimism. Even in high-poverty schools, faculty members' belief in their own ability to effect change and positively influence student learning has a significant correlation with student achievement (Hoy, Sweetland, & Smith, 2002).

When staff willingly collaborate, timely cooperation is also possible. Timely habits of cooperation are the third factor of a strong social system. To successfully automate engagement, strive for frequent short meetings rather than occasional lengthy meetings. Make them positive, make them actionable, and make them inspiring. The following strategies will help you automate engagement among your own staff.

Solutions You Can Use

Run better meetings. Aim to conduct a 20- to 25-minute staff meeting every other week. Set aside five to seven minutes per meeting for teachers to collaborate and share their knowledge. Cultivate a communal flow of knowledge to strengthen connections and foster more informed decision making. Share your best ideas and expect others to do the same; discourage hoarding of expertise! There is a good chance that every teacher has figured out a few things that others have not. Make sure that at each meeting, at least one different teacher shares a strategy success story. When you or faculty share progress and results, be sure to refer to the effort in collective terms: "Our team implemented a total of 36 engagement strategies last week."

Make good use of collaborative time by encouraging staff to focus on important issues rather than trivial ones. Some conversations can take place outside meetings, and some issues can be handled through e-mail. If you communicate to teachers that you value their time, they will make better use of it. Nurturing your staff is like growing a garden: you need to plant seeds (i.e., foster the positive) and pull weeds (i.e., eliminate the negative).

Share and reinforce new staff norms. The words said, actions taken, and decisions made during a staff meeting reveal much about you. Are you constantly defending yourself, or do you listen to feedback? Do you contribute to the collective knowledge base, or do you hoard your best ideas? The best way to automate faculty-wide engagement is to explicitly state and model staff norms that hold everyone—including you—accountable for contributing to a culture of high-quality, serious collaboration. Know these norms inside and out, and make sure the rest of the faculty does, too. The following "Big 5" are a good place to start.

1. Be consistent and dependable. Follow up on what you pledge to do by actually doing it. Start and finish meetings on time.

2. Foster positive intent in yourself and others. Make sure your agenda focuses on student achievement and school success rather than the narrow aim of self-preservation.

3. Cultivate listening skills. Feel safe enough to not feel the need to constantly defend your choices. Instead of using precious time to guard against perceived threats to your positions, put your dukes down and listen carefully. You may find something of value in what others have to say.

4. Build positive relationships. Foster cordiality and collegiality, and discourage the hostile behaviors of blaming, accusing, name-calling, and

suspicion. Make it a habit to say "please," "thank you," and "I'm sorry" when appropriate. These help lubricate communications and open the path to fast solutions.

5. Let go of honest mistakes. Forgive yourself and your colleagues for the occasional misstep. Learn from mistakes, ask "How do we avoid this next time?", and move forward.

To help your school thrive, you need to foster trust, collaboration, and honesty. If any one of those three elements is missing, student achievement will suffer. A staff that works together facilitates information flow, accelerates progress, and helps automate engagement throughout the entire school.

Laying the Groundwork

The strategies in this chapter should enable you to make engagement happen day after day without creating much extra work for yourself. You'll need some momentum to start up the process, but as time goes by, it'll need less maintenance. Best of all, you and your students alike will be less stressed and more engaged.

The final action discussed in this chapter breaks the pattern of the rest of the book by addressing leaders, but it is too important to leave out. Cultivating schoolwide social support will lay the groundwork for all the other actions in this book. Start small, with simple suggestions for collaboration. Success results from the efforts of many; don't try to move mountains by yourself. Use OPB (other people's brains) to generate ideas, implement strategies, analyze results, and solve problems. When trust and collaboration go up, stress and workload go down.

9

"Now What?": Meeting the Challenge of Implementation

In the Classroom

Angela returned from a Title I conference just as the school year began. To say she was excited would be an understatement. When she got the announcement that her school was doing a book study on engagement, her enthusiasm multiplied. She had more ideas than she knew what to do with. Her first week's lesson plan incorporated a whopping 15 new strategies. This was going to be her best year yet!

Matt, a teacher at the same school, had been unable to attend the Title I conference. He knew he needed to do a better job of engaging his own students, so he was mildly encouraged to hear about the book study: this would give him some support. But unlike Angela, Matt liked to do things deliberately, one at a time. Before trying a new strategy, he wanted to know the rationale behind it and make sure it was supported by strong research.

Angela was fueled up and ready to go, like a high-speed train headed out of the station for her destination. Matt knew he had his work cut out for him; he just wanted to think things through and make some decisions for himself.

In your work, you don't need to match Angela's high-energy personality or Matt's reflective personality; it's OK to fall somewhere along the continuum. What *is* important is to take what you've learned and use it to move forward. Accordingly, this chapter addresses the crucial question "How can I successfully implement what I've learned from this book?"

Four Actions for Successful Implementation

This chapter is a little different from the preceding chapters. Instead of focusing on data or research, I have based this chapter on 35 years of my own mistakes. Yes, I admit it: I have made more mistakes as a teacher of both students and adult educators than I'd care to admit. But I learned from those mistakes, and here I share that learning with you.

In this book's Introduction, I mentioned an e-mail I received from a principal at a school with a high student poverty rate whose staff had just finished a book study on *Teaching with Poverty in Mind*. She lamented that her school's achievement scores hadn't improved and asked, "*Now* what do we do?" After some reflection, I replied that she needed to develop a long-term plan to implement the strategies from the book. After all, all a book does is share ideas, findings, strategies, or reflections; it has no intrinsic value. A book's value springs from readers' interaction with the content and with one another—from sharing insights, making decisions, planning new steps, and, ultimately, taking action.

My goal in my own work is to produce miraculous results every day. Sound crazy? Not in the least. Every day, I ask myself, "What can I do better next time?" Some teachers tell me, "I don't know if I can do all this engagement every day. I didn't sign up for this." I advise them to start with taking a small step in the right direction. If you're serious about improving student performance, you must be willing to improve your own performance—no finger pointing and no excuses. I'm sorry if you thought your job should be easy. It's *not* easy to get 100 percent of your students to graduate and have a chance of success in life, but that's what we are paid to do.

Are you willing to take the next step and aim for a higher level of teaching? Are you willing to take the inevitable bumps and bruises you'll get along the way? Are you willing to enrich every single class you teach with powerful learning and engagement? If you are, you'll change your life and the lives of your students.

The four actions laid out in this chapter will support your move toward an exciting yet realistic implementation plan.

Four Actions for Successful Implementation

1. Get organized.
2. Engage with differentiation.
3. Know what to expect.
4. Break down the breakdowns.

Action #1: Get Organized

If you sporadically use a random assortment of this book's strategies in the classroom, their full artistry and potency won't be realized. You must first organize the strategies in meaningful ways that provide immediate cognitive access to all of them. Asking yourself how you can organize these strategies is like asking yourself how to organize music into playlists: there's no single "right" way, just the way that makes sense for you. I like to use the metaphor of Russian nesting dolls: the engagement tools can be organized like the *matryoshka*, with each one nested inside a larger strategy or goal. The following strategies provide some direction for figuring out a system that works quickly and reliably for you.

Solutions You Can Use

Organize strategies by engagement domain. The first step is to identify some main categories of engagement strategies. For example, you could group them according to this book's chapters—a set of strategies that creates a positive climate, another set that elevates energy and focus, a third that deepens students' understanding, and so on. Then ask yourself, "Which system will give me the easiest access to the greatest number of strategies in real time?"

Another starting point is to answer the question "What are the most pressing needs in my classroom?" You might be experiencing problems like

- Insufficient student motivation and effort.
- Slow, frustrated learners.
- Discipline or behavior issues.
- Lack of academic success.

An effective way to organize and address these common issues is through what I call the "Big Four" engagement domains: effort, attitude, behavior, and cognitive capacity (see Figure 9.1).

Figure 9.1 The "Big Four" Engagement Domains

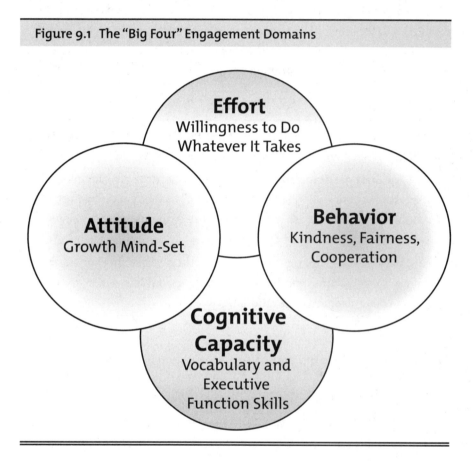

Each domain represents a different facet of school life that teachers deal with every day, and each domain calls for a different type of approach:

- Effort: create a climate that sustains student effort.
- Attitude: build positive attitudes and a growth-oriented, learner's mind-set.
- Behavior: teach and foster behavioral skills that help students learn the importance of kindness, fairness, self-regulation, and cooperation.

- Cognitive capacity: build the cognitive skills to enhance executive function and promote academic success.

You can create a folder for each of these domains and then come up with subfolders describing different needs to be addressed within that domain and containing appropriate strategies. Here's a sample system that organizes strategies from this book by domain and subcategory.

Effort Builders
• **Reinforcement/feedback:** Use emotional punctuation; help students develop and use a rubric; be clear and constructive. • **Student participation:** Pique students' curiosity; ask inclusive questions; ease students in with "bite-size" moves; encourage voluntary hand raising; ask students to share opinions; provide content choice; have students write the rules. • **Classroom climate:** Adopt the "cheerleader" role in your class; ensure equal status; pump up positive classroom responses; use variety in your clapping celebrations.
Attitude Builders
• **Hope and learning mind-set:** Affirm students' ability to learn; affirm students' choices, attitudes, and effort; affirm students' capacity; refer to the learning destination as a certainty; raise students' expectations about their potential to go to college. • **Student energy:** Follow the leader; gallery walk critiques; enlist student teams to conduct energizers; go on a scavenger hunt; cross-laterals. • **Emotional positivity:** Affirm every little success early on; respect your students; upgrade your interactive language; accentuate the positive.

Behavior Builders

- **Appropriate social/emotional responses:** Model appropriate responses; teach responses with fun activities; post and implement participation rules.

- **Mind-body states/classroom rituals:** Reduce lecture time; eliminate the "fight, flight, or freeze" response; give students more control; start class with a ritual; get the class's attention; leave on a high note; celebrate milestones; deal with interruption.

- **Collaboration/cooperation:** Form cooperative groups (elementary); form cooperative teams (secondary); create the "class glue" with get-to-know-you activities; come up with team greetings; let teams take over.

Cognitive Capacity Builders

- **Working memory:** Play recall games; use word baskets and number bags; review increasingly large chunks of content.

- **Attention span:** Increase buy-in; use prediction; pause and chunk; engage in a fast physical activity; get students moving; rhythm claps; balance and point.

- **Self-control:** Use "calendar delays" for classroom question-and-answer time; use the mixed clapping task; teach the power of goals; follow the directions; Simon Says.

Prioritize. As you identify classroom needs or issues that fall under each domain and decide which strategies you'd like to try, remember that there's no single "correct" way to organize the strategies. The system you devise doesn't need to be perfect. You'll probably notice some overlaps across the domains and strategies, and that's OK. The point is to create some clarity in your own mind about what you need to address in the classroom and which direction you should take. You'll end up feeling a greater sense of efficacy and purpose. The worst thing to do would be to try to do too much at once, get overwhelmed, and then just ditch the entire effort.

Once you have identified some issues or needs that fall under each of the Big Four domains and selected their attendant strategies, choose just one domain to work on. I'm serious: focus on one domain for each school year, and work with colleagues who want to implement strategies from the same domain. Collaborate on ways to apply the strategies, review results, tweak and correct your use of them if necessary, and seek out or provide one another with the support necessary to develop mastery. Make it the mission of your professional learning community (PLC) or team to begin small but work purposefully and relentlessly.

KISS every day. Remember the importance of a K-I-S-S: "Keep It Simple, Sweetie." In the context of making changes to your practice, this acronym refers to implementing just one small idea or step at a time.

Do you recall the experience of learning to drive a car? At first, it seemed so overwhelming. You needed to keep your eyes on the road and operate your own vehicle while also predicting other drivers' next moves and continually checking the rear- and side-view mirrors. Yet somehow, with practice, it all came together. Eventually, you were able to carry on a conversation or listen to the radio while driving.

So divide your goals into manageable, bite-size chunks. Keep practicing and refining each chunk until it becomes automatic, and then move on to the next step. Slowly automate these small chunks, and eventually you will have mastered a process or strategy and, eventually, an entire domain, and can use it as seamlessly as you drive your car. At that point, you can move on to the next strategy or domain.

Let's say your team or PLC mission for the year is to build greater student effort. Take a look at the "Effort Builders" section on page 160, which includes three needs to be addressed and actionable strategies to address each one. You can chunk these strategies into even smaller engagement activities: just think of one specific, realistic thing you can try in your classroom today. Here are some examples:

- **Reinforcement/feedback.** *Today's strategy:* Thank students for every contribution they make with a comment like "Thanks very much" or "I appreciate your effort."

- **Student participation.** *Today's strategy:* Show students how to acknowledge one another's participation and effort with a constructive observation like "Your positive attitude really shows, and it's paying off."
- **Classroom climate.** *Today's strategy:* Have each team do its cheer in turn, or give teams three minutes for a quick celebration of their work.

The process of organizing strategies and choosing an initial direction for implementation from any number of possibilities may seem overwhelming, but you can do it. You can master these skills. What you *can't* do is get immediately astounding results. In fact, let's end any delusion that you'll be able to achieve perfection in a week or even a month. The process of becoming an extraordinarily engaging educator is a pathway, not a box to check off on Monday's to-do list. It takes initiative, trial and error, and fine-tuning to master your application of the strategies. In addition, every student is different, and every class has its own personality. The following section will help you shape these strategies to meet different student needs.

Action #2: Engage with Differentiation

Humans share over 99 percent of the same DNA. What makes each of us unique is not just that 1 percent difference in DNA, though; it's a lifetime of experiences that has sculpted each brain into the unique masterpiece that it is.

Just as we are all different, so are our students and their needs. Thus, differentiating instructional and engagement strategies is crucial to your success. Engagement strategies all have the same basic structure. The secret to differentiation is to learn the framework of each strategy, then figure out what to vary to reach every single learner. Soon, you'll have the tools to customize any activity for each student. The following strategies show how you can differentiate any activity with a shift in attitude, application, boundaries, or context.

Solutions You Can Use

Shift your attitude. Broaden your conception of activities' purposes. Don't define a given activity as "for my AD/HD kids," or "just for K–3," or "for a chemistry class." Forget the labels, and forget perfection. Jump in and try something different. Trial and error is your friend as long as you learn from your mistakes. The next time you want to try a new strategy or activity, try this test: ask if you can present it at the next staff meeting. Then ask yourself, "How can I reframe this activity for my *colleagues*?" For example, you could lead faculty in a simple "stand and stretch" routine, or the cross-training simulation described on page 118. By presenting it with enthusiasm and selling it to the staff, you've already started the differentiation process and practiced getting buy-in. Soon, you'll be a pro in repurposing activities for all kinds of contexts.

Keep in mind that your attitude, or mind-set, is the single biggest selling point of your entire repertoire of strategies. A teacher with a fixed mind-set, naturally enough, sees engagement activities as fixed. But a teacher with a growth mind-set sees that all activities share the same basic variables: *application, boundaries,* and *context.* You can alter any or all of these "ABCs" of differentiation to adapt every single activity to your targeted needs. All you need is a little imagination. There is no such thing as a "special education activity" or a "gifted activity." Any activity can work for any age and ability level. By tweaking the ABCs, I have transformed traditional prekindergarten exercises into activities for adults and been met with zero resistance (and, sometimes, with roaring approval). *You* are the primary agent, not the set of directions that came with the activity.

Shift the application. To shift an activity or strategy's application, change *how* you use it. For example, you can turn a math processing activity into a working memory activity by pausing it and asking students to recall the segment (e.g., numbers, key items, or sentences) you just went over. Or try this activity: secretly assign each student a number between 0 and 10, and then divide the class into groups of four to six. Have the students in each group stand in a circle, facing the center, with their hands behind their backs. On your cue ("Throw!"), the students throw their hands in front, revealing with their fingers the number they were assigned. On your next cue ("Shout!"), students must shout out the total number of fingers displayed. This is a processing activity suitable for 3rd graders, but you can turn it into a more complex working memory activity by asking students to put their hands back behind their backs after a short interval and then to recall the number of fingers that each student in the circle displayed.

You can shift activities' applications in other ways, too. For example, for activities that use music, try switching the tempo: play slower music to make the activity more thoughtful or faster music to increase the activity's pace. Speed up any activity, and it becomes an energizer (e.g., play fast music and say, "Touch four tables, four walls, and four chairs. Ready, set, go!"). Slow down the same activity, and it elevates focus (e.g., play slower music and say, "Touch four tables, counting to 10 after each one. At the fourth table, wait for further directions."). When you're finished with an activity, make it more meaningful and extend learning by asking students to debrief it and imagine variations on the activity. They could also discuss the transfer of content or process or make it self-reflective (e.g., "What did this activity teach me about my own memory skills?").

Shift the boundaries. Change the rules of any activity to adapt it to different needs. For example, you can give students additional time to prepare before the activity or to debrief after it, change the number of students in cooperative groups, allow students to look up information or consult a neighbor, turn a team activity into a partner activity, give students a deadline (or remove the deadline), decide what happens when students reach a certain goal, and so on. The possibilities are endless. Whenever an activity gets a bit stale, stop it and let students huddle up and brainstorm new ideas to tweak the activity. At first, give them guidelines. Soon, you'll be getting fresh ideas for variations, and students will be more engaged.

Shift the context. Change the whole set of circumstances for an activity to make it work for different needs. Why not use a morning ritual usually used to start the day as a reward or celebration for finishing early? If you use old material for an activity, call it a review; when you use new material, call it a preview. You can use a given activity near the beginning of the school year to foster collaboration, and reintroduce it later in the year as a competition. There is no shortage of strategies, only creativity. Everything worth using in this book requires a touch of customization, fine-tuning, and automation. Keep the process simple, and effective differentiation will be a reality in your classroom.

Action #3: Know What to Expect

I like to think of this section as "What to Expect When You're Engaging"—a play on the title of Heidi Murkoff's best-selling pregnancy bible *What to Expect When You're Expecting*. Like the long gestation period, the process of increasing engagement can be difficult and sometimes feel endless. But eventually, you get to see the fruit of your labor (pun intended)! This section describes some of what will likely happen as you begin to use the tools in this book. You can expect some bad: lack of support from colleagues, acting out from students, isolation and frustration on your own part. But there's good, too: collegiality, curiosity, and gratification. Expect plenty of bumps in the road to engagement, and stay the course.

Solutions You Can Use

Know what to expect from your students. If you start new initiatives at the beginning of the school year, students will not likely be aware that you're trying something different. But if you make changes to your teaching and engagement strategies during the school year, expect them to notice. They may just be curious and have questions, or they may joke around. Don't get flustered; have a response ready. If they tease, "Looks like *someone* went to another workshop!" tell them, "Yes, I plead guilty to always learning, growing, and hopefully getting better." Or acknowledge their curiosity about the changes by saying, "Things will be different. You'll see some changes, and I think you'll like them." Answer any questions they have. Action #4 (p. 169) goes into more depth on how to respond when a strategy doesn't work well or students challenge you.

Know what to expect from your colleagues. If you are initiating a new engagement approach without staff collaboration, some staff may be skeptical or even critical of your efforts. Certain colleagues may feel threatened: if you become a more engaging teacher, it's harder for them to hide behind the excuse that engagement strategies won't "work" with "these students." There's no need to defend your work to your colleagues. Your results will speak for themselves.

It is better, of course, to work in a collaborative school environment. Your PLC or grade-level or subject-area team can work together on applying this book's ideas. Work cooperatively to take one of the Big Four engagement domains and select or develop a cluster of engagement strategies to incorporate into your teaching. Set a goal of implementing two new strategies every week, using each strategy at least twice. Share your results with colleagues, and set new goals for the following week. Use a password-protected page on the district or school website to post the results of each strategy. Make it a team process that after each teacher posts his or her results for the week, he or she must respond to two others online, so that everyone can see what others are doing. This may seem like too much work at times, but think of it this way: it's *exciting* to be learning, collaborating, and acting as a change agent in your school!

Remember that it's better to under-promise and over-deliver than to bite off more than you can chew and then fall short. Maintain realistic expectations. You'll face obstacles, blunders, and even potential ridicule. Those are normal. Forgive yourself if you slip up, and just keep moving forward. Take baby steps, correct mistakes, and stay away from toxic influences. This is not a sprint; it's a marathon. You can stumble many times and still be a champion at your mission of changing students' lives.

Know what to expect from yourself, and manage your stress. The classic Tony Bennett rendition of the 1959 song "The Best Is Yet to Come" exudes an optimism that is critical for the implementation of any new venture. Why is a positive mind-set so important? Teachers who score high in "life satisfaction," meaning they feel content with their personal and professional lives, are a whopping 43 percent more likely to produce significant achievement gains in the classroom than are their less satisfied colleagues (Duckworth & Quinn, 2009). These teachers spread their zest and enthusiasm to their students, the authors suggest.

Many teachers say that after a restorative summer, their life and career satisfaction erode over the course of the busy school year. This is a wake-up call: if you keep doing the same things that stress you out every school year, every year you'll lose steam after a few months, and you'll get the same result. Assess how well you deal with life and school stressors. If you don't deal with stress in a healthy way, rethink your coping methods and master some new, effective ones.

The way you live your life determines whether you bring yourself and others down or you bring delight to yourself and those around you. There is no school that creates stress; there are only teachers who struggle to handle the stress they generate. Students don't stress you out; *you* stress you out. Take responsibility and stop blaming the administration, your colleagues, your students, the curriculum, or the standards. No one is disputing that teaching well is a tough job; it requires large reserves of resiliency and grit. But stress is not floating in the air like a dust particle. It is your mind and body's response to feeling out of control, and your stress level is largely a function of the strength of your coping skills. The five de-stressing strategies I listed in Chapter 4 (p. 67), slightly tweaked, will work as well for you as for your students. Use these, and you'll reduce the stress and increase the joy in your life.

- Take action by addressing the source of your stress, if appropriate. If you can't address the source right now, focus on what you *can* do.
- Write down the action step to address the source of stress later.
- Use relaxation tools like positive self-talk, mentally reframing the incident, slow breathing, meditation, and yoga.
- Release the stress. Use the one-week rule: if what you're stressed about won't matter in one week, let it go.
- Redirect your energy by working off your stress with exercise or play.

Every time you get frustrated and lose energy, use a positive mental routine to get back on track. Focus on your own personal "carrot" by identifying what motivates you to stay positive and energetic and helps you push through tough days and disappointments. Your carrot might be the good feeling that comes from helping others or the pride you feel in achieving the seemingly impossible. Find ways to measure and track your professional growth—for example, you could ask yourself, "How many strategies did I try out and tweak this month? Am I pursuing my own learning by reading and applying research?" Post a reminder of your goals and progress somewhere you'll see it, such as your refrigerator or your cellphone's memo pad.

Next, create a strong narrative explaining how you'll carry out your plan, and talk it through with a friend or colleague until it feels real. This narrative is important, because your prediction of how your own life will go is one of the strongest predictors of your future. To know your future, create it and reinforce it. Visualize yourself carrying out your goals every day. Keep revisiting the story, three to four times over the course of the year. Here's an idea of what this narrative might look like:

> I'm going to reread Chapter 5 for specific strategies to build students' effort, then consult Chapter 9 for ideas on creating an action plan and organizing my priorities. Next, I'll meet with my PLC to talk about what we'll all be doing. Once everyone's got his or her plan, I'll be charged up and ready to start. I'll start by implementing one new strategy, tweaking it as needed, for two weeks, until I get it working right. Once I've done that, I'll keep implementing something new every two weeks, until my class is awesome. My students will be more engaged, and they'll learn more, too. I expect their scores to go up at least 5 percent this year.

Develop stronger odds for success with if-then action plans so that when a challenge or difficulty arises, you will have already thought through how to respond. Write out key steps or script it out for clarity. Think of responses for "ifs" like the following:

- If I forget what I'm doing in the middle, I will . . .
- If students fade or lose energy, I will . . .
- If a student throws out a wisecrack or a fresh remark about the activity, I will . . .

When you know what to expect and how to respond, discipline problems and student detachment will decrease significantly. Students who are engaged in learning and growing in capacity are less likely to behave inappropriately. You'll come to expect less frustration in your work, and more joy and satisfaction.

Action #4: Break Down the Breakdowns

You'll inevitably experience setbacks on the path to mastery. There will be times when your strategy simply doesn't work, students are confused, and you feel frustrated. Fortunately, long-term success is determined not by how many times you fall but by how many times you get back up and try again differently. Your ongoing learning helps you become great at your job and is a strong contributor to student success.

In his soulful song "Breakdown," musician Jack Johnson yearns for the train he's on to break down so that he can stop to walk and look around: he's craving reflection time. When something does not work, it's important to stop and regroup, break down what went wrong, and fix it. Adaptability and resilience are both huge predictors of teacher success. Nobody ever got good at teaching by avoiding mistakes.

And make no mistake, teaching students from poverty will expose every single weakness in your teaching. They will challenge your expectations of what they are able to accomplish, and if your teaching isn't relevant or engaging, they will let you know through their behavior. You can actually look at this as a good thing: students are a valuable source of feedback on your performance. Everything you get from your students—the rolled eyes, the excitement, the state of apathy, the big smiles—are simply feedback triggered by your actions. Instead of getting upset by negative feedback, change things for next time.

When an activity doesn't work quite right in the classroom, relax; you're bigger than this temporary setback. Try preceding a new strategy with an energizer, or moving more quickly and showing greater passion. We all get better by planning thoughtfully, engaging passionately, and taking risks that might just yield an academic or behavioral miracle. To start this improvement process, you need a way to "break down the breakdowns." The following section will guide you in the process.

Solutions You Can Use

Debrief what happened. When things go wrong, use the following seven-step checklist to examine the variables involved and figure out where the breakdown occurred.

1. Planning: Did you write out the activity or strategy, mentally rehearse it, and prepare any necessary seating arrangements, materials, or music beforehand? Did you plan for any potential modifications needed or for snafus that might occur? Sometimes a strategy doesn't work because it

relies too much on the teacher flying by the seat of his or her pants and not enough on thoughtful planning.

2. Evidence: From the get-go, did you establish a goal and a clear process to evaluate whether you met that goal? What were the actual objectives of the activity? Did you give directions clearly, following the steps in Chapter 2 (p. 31)? Did you communicate and reinforce the goals to your students?

3. Buy-in: Did you get students to care? Did you make the activity relevant, offer enough challenge, and elicit curiosity and anticipation? If you fail to get buy-in, students will often roll their eyes, move slowly, or just flat out resist what you're offering. Remember, their feedback will help you become awesome. Don't blame kids; just ask yourself, "How can I get better buy-in next time?"

4. Difficulty: Was the activity easy to understand and accessible to all students? Did you incrementally increase the level of challenge and offer students choices? Did you provide a way for students to evaluate their performance and correct mistakes?

5. Timing: Was the activity short enough to maintain student energy but long enough to accomplish the goal? Did you allow enough time for students to repeat steps as necessary and build on their learning?

6. Inclusion: Did you find a way to involve everybody? Did you know how to address any lack of student interest? Did you map out a differentiated model to ensure that students at all academic and behavioral levels were able to succeed?

7. Duration/frequency: If the activity was a skill builder, did you use it at least 10 minutes a day, three to five times a week, for one to three months? Did you work with students on their skills not until they got it right, but until they couldn't get it wrong?

Think through next steps. Ineffective teachers try out an idea with little or no preparation. Highly effective teachers think through a strategy with the long term in mind. Once you've analyzed where your strategy or activity went wrong, regroup and start again, focusing on what your students need and planning strategies that will help them succeed.

To plan these next steps, you need to come up with *goal intentions* and *implementation intentions*. Goal intentions specify a certain end point, such as a performance or an outcome: "I aim to reach outcome X." By the time you finish this chapter, come up with a goal intention for your classroom that

• Is directly tied to strengthening purposeful engagement.

• Has a measurable component (e.g., "I will use two new engagers each week").

• Has sufficient clarity (e.g., "I will develop and implement cognitive engagers focused on working memory for 8 to 12 minutes a day, three days a week, using existing content").

• Welcomes accountability and reflection (e.g., "I will post the results on our staff website, read others' comments, and provide a debriefing on the results at our Friday staff meeting").

Whereas goal intentions specify the "what" ("I plan to achieve X"), implementation intentions specify the when, the where, and the how (e.g., "When situation X arises, as I predict it might, I will make response Y"). Implementation intentions incorporate both personal volition (goals) and environmental factors (situations X, Y, or Z) in ways that allow for realistic goal attainment and dramatically boost chances for success (Adriaanse, Gollwitzer, De Ridder, de Wit, & Kroese, 2011). When your strategy or activity breaks down, your implementation intentions will enable you to move on more seamlessly and agilely. Knowing that when you have an unexpected change in your class schedule you can switch from activity X to the less time-consuming activity Y, or that when activity Y doesn't work you can use activity Z, saves you from wasting valuable class time and floundering to figure out a solution in the moment.

Having the Grit to Commit and Raising the Bar

In a recent study (Duckworth & Quinn, 2009), researchers evaluated teachers before and after their first year of teaching. Those who initially scored high for *grit*—defined as toughness, perseverance, and focus on long-term goals—were 31 percent more likely than their lower-scoring peers were to spur solid academic growth in their students. Hard work, passion, and commitment are crucial characteristics for teachers, especially those who teach students living in poverty and other adverse circumstances. It's when things aren't going well that it's most important to square your shoulders, brush off discouragement, and keep going.

If you have made it this far, it's decision time. Whether you read this book on your own or as part of a professional development book study, you must answer a simple question: are you in or out? Do you have the grit to commit to the success of your students without making excuses? Or will you set this book down and say, "Maybe I'll get around to this stuff someday"? I hope you'll embrace the possibilities and start today. Set your personal bar higher.

Trying out new ideas and stretching my potential is the most satisfying part of my job; I love this work, even when I stumble. It wasn't always this way, though. Some years after I left the classroom, I became a staff developer. In the beginning, my own performance bar was set so low that my main goal was *not* getting a ton of negative feedback. After years of trial and error (and subsequent error correction), I began to enjoy days with plenty of positive feedback. However, I never had a glimpse of just how well I could do until one day when everything just came together perfectly. I was working all day with a group of 200 educators, and my presentation was clear and crisp; I felt so focused and thoroughly enthusiastic. At 11:30 a.m., I asked the group to stand up to head out for lunch. At that unlikely moment, they stopped what they were doing and gave me a spontaneous standing ovation. My eyes welled up with humility. I had reached a new level of job performance that, ever since, I have strived to reach every workday.

I'm not recounting this story to brag. The episode is stuck in my memory because I am constantly learning and trying to do better. I probably read 200 to 300 peer-reviewed studies a year. Not long ago, I was catching up on research and found some compelling studies on staff development that described factors influencing the likelihood that content or skills will be implemented in schools. What I read was sobering and suggested that in some ways, I am still a beginner with many more hills to climb. Once again, I raised the bar and set my sights higher. If I allow myself to become complacent, my chances of getting another standing ovation are slim.

We all have to start setting our personal bars much higher. *Welcome* the challenges presented by this book; find a starting place and pick a strategy to try. Get together with your team and start changing lives. If you have issues at home, we understand. If you have issues with colleagues, we understand. But none of your issues gives you the right to hurt a single kid's chances for graduation. Never make students the victims of your unwillingness to make changes in yourself.

Sometimes we're reluctant to change ourselves out of fear of risk or loss. But although taking risks may result in failure, not taking risks *guarantees* failure. If you refuse to try new things, you rob both your students of their possibilities and you of your own potential. Fear is normal, but it must be managed. Marianne Williamson (1996), a spiritual teacher, writes about fear quite well:

> Our deepest fear is not that we are inadequate.
> Our deepest fear is that we are powerful beyond measure.
>
> It is our light, not our darkness that most frightens us.
> We ask ourselves, "Who am I to be brilliant,
> gorgeous, talented and fabulous?"
> Actually, who are you not to be?
>
> You are a child of God.
> Your playing small doesn't serve the world.
> There is nothing enlightened about shrinking so that
> other people won't feel insecure around you.
>
> We were born to manifest the Glory of God within us.
> It's not just in some of us; it's in everyone.
> As we let our own light shine, we unconsciously
> give other people permission to do the same.
> As we are liberated from our own fear,
> our presence automatically liberates others. (p. 191)

Whether or not you believe in a religious God is less important than the questions Williamson asks. How can you be in teaching and *not* give your students everything you've got?

Your Next Step

Every student in your school would rather be engaged by an energetic, caring teacher than be bored by someone going through the motions. Kids deserve a great day *every* day. They need role models. They need caring adults. They need savvy risk takers who aren't afraid to fail. If you're not modeling those qualities, where will your students learn them? If you're thinking this sounds impossible, maybe a little practice would expand your conception of what is possible. A conversation between Alice and the White Queen in *Alice's Adventures in Wonderland* (Carroll, 1993) comes to mind:

> Alice laughed. "There's no use trying," she said: "one *can't* believe impossible things."
>
> "I daresay you haven't had much practice," said the Queen. "When I was your age, I always did it for half-an-hour a day. Why, sometimes I've believed as many as six impossible things before breakfast." (p. 37)

For impossible things to happen, you have to envision them first. It's up to you. Miracles will happen in your classroom when you build your dreams bigger than your challenges. Are students not trying hard enough? Reread Chapter 5 and build their motivation and effort. Is there too much "sit and git" in your class? Reread Chapter 7 and increase students' energy and focus. You can achieve miracles, but you have to go after them yourself.

A "no excuses" mentality means that even if you believe it *should* be students' job to be engaged, you *accept* that it's your job to engage them. Engaging students is not just part of your obligation to be a good teacher: our country's economic, social, and cultural survival relies on it. For every additional 1 percent of students who graduate, we are all better off. Higher graduation rates are correlated with lower unemployment, smaller prison populations, fewer adults receiving government services, more marriages that last, more adults paying taxes, and, ultimately, a more prosperous country (Heckman, Humphries, & Mader, 2011).

Alter your life course today. Destiny is not fixed. The students in your class may be future doctors, activists, engineers, Nobel laureates, teachers, or presidents—*if* they believe that they really can learn. The upcoming school year might be the year when a few students decide whether they will stay in school or drop out and become a drain on society. They deserve nothing less than your best effort.

I opened this book with the story of a kid—me—who struggled in school. I earned poor grades and I disengaged, but a middle school teacher cared enough to connect with me and build my effort, attitude, behavior, and cognitive capacity. That teacher made all the difference in my life. Can you be that miracle teacher for your class this year? Will you try? Your students await your answer.

References

Aberg, M. A., Pedersen, N. L., Toren, K., Svartengren, M., Backstrand, B., Johnsson, T., et al. (2009). Cardiovascular fitness is associated with cognition in young adulthood. *Proceedings of the National Academy of Sciences of the United States of America [USA], 106*(49), 20906–20911.

Ackerman, B. P., & Brown, E. D. (2006). Income poverty, poverty co-factors, and the adjustment of children in elementary school. *Advances in Child Development and Behavior, 34,* 91–129.

Adolphs, R. (2003). Cognitive neuroscience of human social behaviour. *Nature Reviews Neuroscience, 4*(3), 165–178.

Adriaanse, M. A., Gollwitzer, P. M., De Ridder, D. T., de Wit, J. B., & Kroese, F. M. (2011). Breaking habits with implementation intentions: A test of underlying processes. *Personal Social Psychology Bulletin, 37*(4), 502–513.

Alliance for Excellent Education. (2008). *Students of color and the achievement gap.* Washington, DC: Author. Available: http://www.all4ed.org/about_the_crisis/students/students_of_color

Alloway, T. P., & Alloway, R. G. (2010). Investigating the predictive roles of working memory and IQ in academic attainment. *Journal of Experimental Child Psychology, 106*(1), 20–29.

Alloway, T. P., Gathercole, S. E., Kirkwood, H., & Elliott, J. (2009). The cognitive and behavioral characteristics of children with low working memory. *Child Development, 80*(2), 606–621.

Almeida, D. M., Neupert, S. D., Banks, S. R., & Serido, J. (2005). Do daily stress processes account for socioeconomic health disparities? *Journals of Gerontology Series B—Psychological Sciences and Social Sciences, 60*(2), S34–S39.

Amat, J. A., Bansal, R., Whiteman, R., Haggerty, R., Royal, J., & Peterson, B. S. (2008). Correlates of intellectual ability with morphology of the hippocampus and amygdala in healthy adults. *Brain and Cognition, 66*(2), 105–114.

Appleton, J. J., Christenson, S. L., & Furlong, M. J. (2008). Student engagement with school: Critical conceptual and methodological issues of the construct. *Psychology in the Schools, 45,* 369–386.

Argyropoulos, G. P., & Muggleton, N. G. (2013). Effects of cerebellar stimulation on processing semantic associations. *Cerebellum, 12*(1), 83–96.

Ariga, A., & Lleras, A. (2011, January 4). Brief and rare mental "breaks" keep you focused: Deactivation and reactivation of task goals preempt vigilance decrements. *Cognition, 118*(3), 439–443.

Attar, B. K., Guerra, N. G., & Tolan, P. H. (1994). Neighborhood disadvantage, stressful life events, and adjustment in urban elementary-school children. *Journal of Clinical Child Psychology, 23*, 391–400.

Barrouillet, P., & Lecas, J. F. (1999). Mental models in conditional reasoning and working memory. *Thinking and Reasoning, 5*, 289–302.

Barton, P. E. (2005). *One-third of a nation: Rising dropout rates and declining opportunities.* Princeton, NJ: Educational Testing Service.

Basch, C. E. (2011). Breakfast and the achievement gap among urban minority youth. *Journal of School Health, 81*, 635–640.

Baydar, N., Brooks-Gunn, J., & Furstenberg, F. (1993). Early warning signs of functional illiteracy: Predictors in childhood and adolescence. *Child Development, 64*(3), 815–829.

Belsky, J., Pasco Fearon, R. M., & Bell, B. (2007). Parenting, attention and externalizing problems: Testing mediation longitudinally, repeatedly and reciprocally. *Journal of Child Psychology and Psychiatry, 48*(12), 1233–1242.

Bequet, F., Gomez-Merino, D., Berthelot, M., & Guezennec, C. Y. (2001). Exercise-induced changes in brain glucose and serotonin revealed by microdialysis in rat hippocampus: Effect of glucose supplementation. *Acta Physiologica Scandinavica, 173*(2), 223–230.

Bernstein, J., Mishel, L., & Boushey, H. (2002). *The state of working America 2002–03.* Washington, DC: Economic Policy Institute.

Bishaw, A., & Renwick, T. J. (2009). *Poverty: 2007 and 2008 American community surveys.* Washington, DC: U.S. Census Bureau. Available: http://www.census.gov/prod/2009pubs/acsbr08-1.pdf

Black, A. E., & Deci, E. L. (2000). The effects of instructors' autonomy support and students' autonomous motivation on learning organic chemistry: A self-determination theory perspective. *Science Education, 84*, 740–756.

Blackwell, L. S., Trzesniewski, K. H., & Dweck, C. S. (2007). Implicit theories of intelligence predict achievement across an adolescent transition: A longitudinal study and an intervention. *Child Development, 78*, 263.

Bolland, L., Lian, B. E., & Formichella, C. M. (2005). The origins of hopelessness among inner-city African-American adolescents. *American Journal of Community Psychology, 36*(3/4), 293–305.

Bracey, G. W. (2006). Poverty's infernal mechanism. *Principal Leadership, 6*(6), 60.

Bradley, R. H., & Corwyn, R. F. (2002, February). Socioeconomic status and child development. *Annual Review of Psychology, 53*, 371–399.

Bradley, R. H., Corwyn, R. F., Burchinal, M., McAdoo, H. P., & Coll, C. G. (2001). The home environments of children in the United States, Part II: Relations with behavioral development through age thirteen. *Child Development, 72*(6), 1868–1886.

Brooks-Gunn, J., Guo, G., & Furstenberg, F. (1993). Who drops out of and who continues beyond high school? *Journal of Research on Adolescence, 3*(3), 271–294.

Brophy, J. E. (2004). *Motivating students to learn*. Mahwah, NJ: Erlbaum.

Bryk, A. S. (2010). Organizing schools for improvement. *Phi Delta Kappan, 91*(7), 23–30.

Buschkuehl, M., & Jaeggi, S. M. (2010). Improving intelligence: A literature review. *Swiss Medical Weekly, 140*(19–20), 266–272.

Carbon, C. C. (2011). The first 100 milliseconds of a face: On the microgenesis of early face processing. *Perceptual and Motor Skills, 113*(3), 859–874.

Carey, K. (2005). *The funding gap 2004: Many states still shortchange low-income and minority students*. Washington, DC: Education Trust.

Carleton, L., & Marzano, R. J. (2010). *Vocabulary games for the classroom*. Centennial, CO: Marzano Research Laboratory.

Carroll, L. (1993). *Alice's adventures in Wonderland*. New York: Dover.

Casey, B., Somerville, L., Gotlib, I., Ayduk, O., Franklin, N., Askren, M., et al. (2011). Behavioral and neural correlates of delay of gratification 40 years later. *Proceedings of the National Academy of Sciences of the USA, 108*(36), 14998–15003.

Castelli, D., Hillman, C., Buck, S., & Erwin, H. (2007). Physical fitness and academic achievement in third- and fifth-grade students. *Journal of Sport & Exercise, 29*, 239–252.

Castiello, U., Becchio, C., Zoia, S., Nelini, C., Sartori, L., Blason, L., et al. (2010). Wired to be social: The ontogeny of human interaction. *PLoS ONE, 5*(10), e13199.

Catalino, L. I., & Fredrickson, B. L. (2011). A Tuesday in the life of a flourisher: The role of positive emotional reactivity in optimal mental health. *Emotion, 11*(4), 938–950.

Chapman, C., Laird, J., Ifill, N., & KewalRamani, A. (2011). *Trends in high school dropout and completion rates in the United States: 1972–2009* (NCES 2012-006). Washington, DC: National Center for Education Statistics. Available: http://nces.ed.gov/pubs2012/2012006.pdf

Chesebro, J. L. (2003). Effects of teaching clarity and nonverbal immediacy on student learning, receiver apprehension, and affect. *Communication Education, 52*(2), 135–147.

Coe, R. (2002, September 12–14). *It's the effect size, stupid: What effect size is and why it is important*. Paper presented at the Annual Conference of the British Educational Research Association, University of Exeter, England.

Coleman-Jensen, A., Nord, M., Andrews, M., & Carlson, S. (2011, September). *Household food security in the United States in 2010*. Economic Research Report No. ERR-125. Washington, DC: Economic Research Service, United States Department of Agriculture. Available: http://www.ers.usda.gov/publications/err-economic-research-report/err125.aspx#.UVB-NXCrUmk

Compton-Lilly, C. (2003). *Reading families: The literate lives of urban children*. New York: Teachers College Press.

Cornelius-White, J., & Harbaugh, A. (2010). *Learner-centered instruction: Building relationships for student success*. Thousand Oaks, CA: Sage.

Croizet, J., & Claire, T. (1998). Extending the concept of stereotype threat to social class: The intellectual underperformance of students from low socioeconomic backgrounds. *Personality and Social Psychology Bulletin, 24*(6), 588–594.

Daneman, M., & Carpenter, P. A. (1980). Individual differences in working memory and reading. *Journal of Verbal Learning and Verbal Behavior, 19*, 450–466.

De Smedt, B., Janssen, R., Bouwens, K., Verschaffel, L., Boets, B., & Ghesquière, P. (2009). Working memory and individual differences in mathematics achievement: A longitudinal study from first grade to second grade. *Journal of Experimental Child Psychology, 103*(2), 186–201.

Deci, E. L., Koestner, R., & Ryan, M. R. (1999). A meta-analytic review of experiments examining the effects of extrinsic rewards on intrinsic motivation. *Psychological Bulletin, 125*, 627–668.

Dimberg, U., & Thunberg, M. (1998). Rapid facial reactions to emotional facial expressions. *Scandinavian Journal of Psychology, 39*(1), 39–45.

Donnelly, J. E., & Lambourne, K. (2011). Classroom-based physical activity, cognition, and academic achievement. *Preventative Medicine, 52* (Supplement 1), S36–42.

Douglas-Hall, A., & Chau, M. (2007). *Most low-income parents are employed.* New York: National Center for Children in Poverty. Available: http://www.nccp.org/publications /pdf/text_784.pdf

Driemeyer, J., Boyke, J., Gaser, C., Büchel, C., & May, A. (2008). Changes in gray matter induced by learning—revisited. *PLoS ONE, 3*(7), e2669.

Duckworth, A. L., & Quinn, P. D. (2009). Development and validation of the short grit scale (grit-s). *Journal of Personal Assessment, 91*(2), 166–174.

Duncan, G. J., Brooks-Gunn, J., & Klebanov, P. K. (1994). Economic deprivation and early childhood development. *Child Development, 65*, 296–318.

Duyme, M., Dumaret, A. C., & Tomkiewicz, S. (1999). How can we boost IQs of "dull children"? A late adoption study. *Proceedings of the National Academy of Sciences of the USA, 96*(15), 8790–8794.

Dweck, C. (2006). *Mindset: The new psychology of success.* New York: Ballentine.

Eichenbaum, H. (2004). Hippocampus: Cognitive processes and neural representations that underlie declarative memory. *Neuron, 44*, 109–120.

Eisenberger, N. I., Jarcho, J. M., Lieberman, M. D., & Naliboff, B. D. (2006). An experimental study of shared sensitivity to physical pain and social rejection. *Pain, 126*(1–3), 132–138.

Ekman, P. (2004). *Emotions revealed: Recognizing faces and feelings to improve communication and personal life.* New York: Holt.

Elliott, J., Gathercole, S. E., Alloway, T. P., Holmes, J., & Kirkwood, H. (2010). An evaluation of a classroom-based intervention to help overcome working memory difficulties and improve long-term academic achievement. *Journal of Cognitive Education and Psychology, 9*, 227–250.

Emery, R. E., & Laumann-Billings, L. (1998). An overview of the nature, causes, and consequences of abusive family relationships: Toward differentiating maltreatment and violence. *American Psychologist, 53*, 121–135.

Erickson, K., Drevets, W., & Schulkin, J. (2003). Glucocorticoid regulation of diverse cognitive functions in normal and pathological emotional states. *Neuroscience and Biobehavioral Reviews, 27,* 233–246.

Evans, G. W. (2003). A multimethodological analysis of cumulative risk and allostatic load among rural children. *Developmental Psychology, 39*(5), 924–933.

Evans, G. W. (2004). The environment of childhood poverty. *American Psychologist, 59,* 77–92.

Evans, G. W., & Kim, P. (2012). Childhood poverty and young adults' allostatic load: The mediating role of childhood cumulative risk exposure. *Psychological Science, 23*(9), 979–983.

Evans, G. W., Kim, P., Ting, A. H., Tesher, H. B., & Shannis, D. (2007). Cumulative risk, maternal responsiveness, and allostatic load among young adolescents. *Developmental Psychology, 43*(2), 341–351.

Evans, G. W., & Schamberg, M. A. (2009). Childhood poverty, chronic stress, and adult working memory. *Proceedings of the National Academy of Sciences of the USA, 106*(16), 6545–6549.

Evans, G. W., Wells, N. M., & Moch, A. (2003). Housing and mental health: A review of the evidence and a methodological and conceptual critique. *Journal of Social Issues, 59*(3), 475–500.

Feduccia, A. A., & Duvauchelle, C. L. (2008). Auditory stimuli enhance MDMA-conditioned reward and MDMA-induced nucleus accumbens dopamine, serotonin and locomotor responses. *Brain Research Bulletin, 77*(4), 189–196.

Fields, J. (2004). *Current population reports: America's families and living arrangements.* Washington, DC: U.S. Census Bureau. Available: http://www.census.gov/prod/2004pubs/p20-553.pdf

Fields, J., & Casper, L. M. (2001). *Current population reports: America's families and living arrangements.* Washington, DC: U.S. Census Bureau.

Finn, J. D., & Rock, D. A. (1997). Academic success among students at risk for school failure. *Journal of Applied Psychology, 82*(2), 221–234.

Fredrickson, B. L., & Branigan, C. (2005). Positive emotions broaden the scope of attention and thought-action repertoires. *Cognition and Emotion, 19,* 313–332.

Fredrickson, B. L., & Joiner, T. (2002). Positive emotions trigger upward spirals toward emotional well-being. *Psychological Science, 13*(2), 172–175.

Fredrickson, B. L., Tugade, M. M., Waugh, C. E., & Larkin, G. R. (2003). What good are positive emotions in crises? A prospective study of resilience and emotions following the terrorist attacks on the United States on September 11th, 2001. *Journal of Personality & Social Psychology, 84*(2), 365–376.

Fukuda, K., & Vogel, E. K. (2009). Human variation in overriding attentional capture. *Journal of Neuroscience, 29,* 8726–8733.

Gershoff, E. T. (2002). Corporal punishment by parents and associated child behaviors and experiences: A meta-analytic and theoretical review. *Psychological Bulletin, 128*(4), 539–579.

Ghaith, G. M. (2002). The relationship between cooperative learning, perception of social support, and academic achievement. *System, 30,* 263–273.

Gianaros, P. J., Horenstein, J. A., Hariri, A. R., Sheu, L. K., Manuck, S. B., Matthews, K. A., et al. (2008). Potential neural embedding of parental social standing. *Social Cognitive and Affective Neuroscience, 3*(2), 91–96.

Gillberg, M., Anderzen, I., Akerstedt, T., & Sigurdson, K. (1986). Urinary catecholamine responses to basic types of physical activity. *European Journal of Applied Physiology, 55,* 575–578.

Ginsberg, S. M. (2007). Teacher transparency: What students can see from faculty communication. *Journal of Cognitive Affective Learning, 4*(1), 13–24.

Gobet, F., & Clarkson, G. (2004). Chunks in expert memory: Evidence for the magical number four . . . or is it two? *Memory, 12*(6), 732–747.

Gómez-Pinilla, F. (2008). Brain foods: The effects of nutrients on brain function. *Nature Reviews Neuroscience, 9*(7), 568–578.

Gonzalez, V. (2005). Cultural, linguistic, and socioeconomic factors influencing monolingual and bilingual children's cognitive development. In V. Gonzalez & J. Tinajero (Eds.), *Review of research and practice* (Vol. 3) (pp. 67–104). Mahwah, NJ: Erlbaum.

Gorski, P. (2008). The myth of the culture of poverty. *Educational Leadership, 65*(7), 32–36.

Gottlieb, D. J., Beiser, A. S., & O'Connor, G. T. (1995). Poverty, race, and medication use are correlates of asthma hospitalization rates: A small area analysis in Boston. *Chest, 108*(1), 28–35.

Hackman, D. A., & Farah, M. J. (2009). Socioeconomic status and the developing brain. *Trends in Cognitive Sciences, 13*(2), 65–73.

Hammack, P. L., Robinson, W. L., Crawford, I., & Li, S. T. (2004). Poverty and depressed mood among urban African-American adolescents: A family stress perspective. *Journal of Child and Family Studies, 13*(3), 309–323.

Hamre, B. K., & Pianta, R. C. (2001). Early teacher-child relationships and the trajectory of children's school outcomes through eighth grade. *Child Development, 72*(2), 625–638.

Hanson, J. L., Chandra, A., Wolfe, B. L., & Pollak, S. D. (2011). Association between income and the hippocampus. *PLoS ONE, 6*(5), e18712.

Hanushek, E. (2005). The economics of school quality. *German Economic Review, 6*(3), 269–286.

Hart, B., & Risley, T. R. (1995). *Meaningful differences in the everyday experience of young American children.* Baltimore: Brookes.

Hart, B., & Risley, T. R. (2003). The early catastrophe: The 30 million word gap by age 3. *American Educator, 27*(1), 4–9.

Hattie, J. (2003, October). *Teachers make a difference: What is the research evidence?* Presentation at the Australian Council for Educational Research Annual Conference on Building Teacher Quality, Melbourne, Australia.

Hattie, J. (2008). *Visible learning: A synthesis of over 800 meta-analyses relating to achievement.* New York: Routledge.

Hattie, J. (2011). *Visible learning for teachers: Maximizing impact on learning.* New York: Routledge.

Hattie, J., & Timperley, H. (2007). The power of feedback. *Review of Educational Research, 1*(77), 81–112.

Haystead, M. W., & Marzano, R. J. (2009). *Meta-analytic synthesis of studies conducted at Marzano Research Laboratory on Instructional Strategies.* Bloomington, IN: Marzano Research Laboratory.

Heckman, J., Humphries, J., & Mader, N. (2011). The GED. In E. Hanushek, S. Machin, & L. Woessman (Eds.), *Handbook of the economics of education* (Vol. 3) (pp. 423–483). Amsterdam: Elsevier.

Henry, P. C. (2005). Life stress, explanatory style, hopelessness, and occupational stress. *International Journal of Stress Management, 12,* 241–256.

Hernandez, D. (2012). *Double jeopardy: How third-grade reading skills and poverty influence high school graduation.* Baltimore: Annie E. Casey Foundation. Available: http://www. aecf.org/~/media/Pubs/Topics/Education/Other/DoubleJeopardyHowThirdGrade ReadingSkillsandPovery/DoubleJeopardyReport040511FINAL.pdf

Hillman, C., Buck, S., Themanson, J., Pontifex, M., & Castelli, D. (2009). Aerobic fitness and cognitive development: Event-related brain potential and task performance indices of executive control in preadolescent children. *Developmental Psychology, 45*(1), 114–129.

Hiroto, D. S., & Seligman, M. E. P. (1975). Generality of learned helplessness in man. *Journal of Personality and Social Psychology, 31,* 311–327.

Hoff, E. (2003). The specificity of environmental influence: Socioeconomic status affects early vocabulary development via maternal speech. *Child Development, 74,* 1368–1378.

Holmes, J., Gathercole, S. E., Place, M., Dunning, D. L., Hilton, K. A., & Elliott, J. G. (2010). Working memory deficits can be overcome: Impacts of training and medication on working memory in children with ADHD. *Applied Cognitive Psychology, 24,* 827–836.

Hoy, W. K., Sweetland, S. R., & Smith, P. A. (2002). Toward an organizational model of achievement in high schools: The significance of collective efficacy. *Educational Administration Quarterly, 38,* 77–93.

Hoy, W. K., Tarter, C. J., & Woolfolk-Hoy, A. (2006). Academic optimism of schools. In W. K. Hoy & C. Miskel (Eds.), *Contemporary issues in educational policy and school outcomes* (pp. 135–156). Greenwich, CT: Information Age.

Izard, C. E., Fine, S. A., Schultz, D., Mostow, A., Ackerman, B. P., & Youngstrom, E. A. (2001). Emotion knowledge as a predictor of social behavior and academic competence in children at risk. *Psychological Science, 12,* 18–23.

Jaeggi, S. M., Buschkuehl, M., Jonides, J., & Perrig, W. J. (2008). Improving fluid intelligence with training on working memory. *Proceedings of the National Academy of Sciences of the USA, 105*(19), 6829–6833.

Jensen, E. (2003). *Tools for engagement.* Thousand Oaks, CA: Corwin Press.

Jensen, E., & Nickelsen, L. (2008). *Deeper learning.* Thousand Oaks, CA: Corwin Press.

Jiang, J., Scolaro, A. J., Bailey, K., & Chen, A. (2011). The effect of music-induced mood on attentional networks. *International Journal of Psychology, 46*(3), 214–222.

Jing, L., & Xudong, W. (2008). Evaluation on the effects of relaxing music on the recovery from aerobic exercise-induced fatigue. *Journal of Sports Medicine and Physical Fitness, 48*(1), 102–106.

Job, V., Dweck, C. S., & Walton, G. M. (2010). Ego depletion—Is it all in your head? Implicit theories about willpower affect self-regulation. *Psychological Science, 21*(11), 1686–1693.

Johnson, D. S. (1981). Naturally acquired learned helplessness: The relationship of school failure to achievement behavior, attributions, and self-concept. *Journal of Educational Psychology, 73*(2), 174–180.

Johnson, D. W., & Johnson, R. (1999). *Learning together and alone: Cooperative, competitive, and individualistic learning* (5th ed.). Boston: Allyn and Bacon.

Johnston-Brooks, C. H., Lewis, M. A., Evans, G. W., & Whalen, C. K. (1998). Chronic stress and illness in children: The role of allostatic load. *Psychosomatic Medicine, 60*(5), 597–603.

Jordan, A. H., Monin, B., Dweck, C. S., Lovett, B. J., John, O. P., & Gross, J. J. (2011, January). Misery has more company than people think: Underestimating the prevalence of others' negative emotions. *Personality & Social Psychology Bulletin, 37*(1), 120–135.

Kapp, K. (2012). *The gamification of learning and instruction.* San Francisco: Wiley and Sons.

Karoly, L. A. (2001). Investing in the future: Reducing poverty through human capital investments. In S. Danzinger & R. Haveman (Eds.), *Understanding poverty* (pp. 314–356). New York: Russell Sage Foundation.

Kitamura, T., Mishina, M., & Sugiyama, H. (2006). Dietary restriction increases hippocampal neurogenesis by molecular mechanisms independent of NMDA receptors. *Neuroscience Letters, 393*(2–3), 94–96.

Klingberg, T., Fernell, E., Olesen, P. J., Johnson, M., Gustafsson, P., Dahlström, K., et al. (2005). Computerized training of working memory in children with ADHD—A randomized, controlled trial. *Journal of the American Academy of Child & Adolescent Psychiatry, 44*(2), 177–186.

Kosfeld, M., Heinrichs, M., Zak, P. J., Fischbacher, U., & Fehr, E. (2005). Oxytocin increases trust in humans. *Nature, 435*(2), 673–676.

Kozorovitskiy, Y., & Gould, E. (2004). Dominance hierarchy influences adult neurogenesis in the dentate gyrus. *Journal of Neuroscience, 24*(30), 6755–7659.

Kraus, M. W., Piff, P. K., & Keltner, D. (2009). Social class, sense of control, and social explanation. *Journal of Personality and Social Psychology, 97*(6), 992–1004.

Krause, C. (2011). Developing sense of coherence in educational contexts: Making progress in promoting mental health in children. *International Review of Psychiatry, 23*(6), 525–532.

Kulik, J. (1998). *Curriculum tracks and high school vocational studies.* Ann Arbor, MI: University of Michigan.

Larmer, J., & Mergendoller, J. R. (2010). Seven essentials for project-based learning. *Educational Leadership, 68*(1), 34–37.

Leuner, B., Caponiti, J. M., & Gould, E. (2012). Oxytocin stimulates adult neurogenesis even under conditions of stress and elevated glucocorticoids. *Hippocampus, 22*(4), 861–868.

Liaw, F. R., & Brooks-Gunn, J. (1994). Cumulative familial risks and low-birthweight children's cognitive and behavioral development. *Journal of Clinical Child Psychology, 23*(4), 360–372.

Lichter, D. T. (1997, August). Poverty and inequality among children. *Annual Review of Sociology, 23*, 121–145.

Lindsey, R. B., Karns, M. S., & Myatt, K. T. (2010). *Culturally proficient education: An asset-based response to conditions of poverty*. Thousand Oaks, CA: Corwin Press.

Luby, J. L., Barch, D. M., Belden, A., Gaffrey, M. S., Tillman, R., Babb, C., et al. (2012). Maternal support in early childhood predicts larger hippocampal volumes at school age. *Proceedings of the National Academy of Sciences of the USA, 109*(8), 2854–2859.

Malatesta, C. Z., & Izard, C. E. (1984). The facial expression of emotion: Young, middle-aged, and older adult expressions. In C. Z. Malatesta & C. E. Izard (Eds.), *Emotion in adult development* (pp. 253–273). Beverly Hills, CA: Sage.

Maldonado-Carreño, C., & Votruba-Drzal, E. (2011). Teacher-child relationships and the development of academic and behavioral skills during elementary school: A within- and between-child analysis. *Child Development, 82*(2), 601–616.

Mangels, J. A., Butterfield, B., Lamb, J., Good, C., & Dweck, C. S. (2006). Why do beliefs about intelligence influence learning success? A social cognitive neuroscience model. *Social Cognitive and Affective Neuroscience, 1*(2), 75–86.

Marks, H. (2000). Student engagement in instructional activity: Patterns in the elementary, middle, and high school years. *American Educational Research Journal, 37*(1), 153–184.

McDonough, C., Song, L., Hirsh-Pasek, K., Golinkoff, R. M., & Lannon, R. (2011). An image is worth a thousand words: Why nouns tend to dominate verbs in early word learning. *Developmental Science, 14*(2), 181–189.

McLoyd, V. C. (1998). Socioeconomic disadvantage and child development. *American Psychologist, 53*(2), 185–204.

Menyuk, P. (1980). Effect of persistent otitis media on language development. *Annals of Otology, Rhinology, and Laryngology Supplement, 89*(3), 257–263.

Miller, E. M., Walton, G. M., Dweck, C. S., Job, V., Trzesniewski, K. H., & McClure, S. M. (2012). Theories of willpower affect sustained learning. *PLoS ONE, 7*(6), e38680.

Mischel, W., Shoda, Y., & Rodriguez, M. (1989). Delay of gratification in children. *Science, 244*(4907), 933–938.

Myers, S. A., & Knox, R. L. (2001). The relationship between college student information-seeking behaviors and perceived instructor verbal behaviors. *Communication Education, 50*(4), 343–356.

Niederer, I., Kriemler, S., Gut, J., Hartmann, T., Schindler, C., Barral, J., et al. (2011). Relationship of aerobic fitness and motor skills with memory and attention in preschoolers (Ballabeina): A cross-sectional and longitudinal study. *BMC Pediatrics, 11*, 34.

Noble, K. G., Norman, M. F., & Farah, M. J. (2005). Neurocognitive correlates of socioeconomic status in kindergarten children. *Developmental Science, 8*(1), 74–87.

Oberle, E., Schonert-Reichl, K. A., Lawlor, M. S., & Thomson, K. C. (2012). Mindfulness and inhibitory control in early adolescence. *Journal of Early Adolescence, 4*(32), 565–588.

Odéen, M., Westerlund, H., Theorell, T., Leineweber, C., Eriksen, H. R., & Ursin, H. (2013). Expectancies, socioeconomic status, and self-rated health: Use of the simplified TOMCATS questionnaire. *International Journal of Behavioral Medicine, 20*(2), 242–251.

O'Malley, G. (2011). Aerobic exercise enhances executive function and academic achievement in sedentary, overweight children aged 7–11 years. *Journal of Physiotherapy, 57*(4), 255.

Pascarella, E. T., Salisbury, M. H., & Blaich, C. F. (2009, November). *Exposure to effective instruction and college student persistence: A multi-institutional replication and extension.* Paper presented at the annual conference of the Association for the Study of Higher Education, Vancouver, British Columbia, Canada.

Patall, E. A., Cooper, H., & Robinson, J. C. (2008). The effects of choice on intrinsic motivation and related outcomes: A meta-analysis of research findings. *Psychological Bulletin, 134,* 270–300.

Patall, E. A., Cooper, H., & Wynn, S. R. (2010). The effectiveness and relative importance of providing choices in the classroom. *Journal of Educational Psychology, 102,* 896–915.

Paul, G., Elam, B., & Verhulst, S. J. (2007). A longitudinal study of students' perceptions of using deep breathing meditation to reduce testing stresses. *Teaching and Learning in Medicine, 19*(3), 287–292.

Pereira, A. C., Huddleston, D. E., Brickman, A. M., Sosunov, A. A., Hen, R., McKhann, G. M., et al. (2007). An in vivo correlate of exercise-induced neurogenesis in the adult dentate gyrus. *Proceedings of the National Academy of Sciences of the USA, 104*(13), 5638–5643.

Persson, M. L., Wasserman, D., Geijer, T., Frisch, A., Rockah, R., Michaelovsky, E., et al. (2000). Dopamine D4 receptor gene polymorphism and personality traits in healthy volunteers. *European Archives of Psychiatry and Clinical Neuroscience, 250*(4), 203–206.

Pianta, R. C., Belsky, J., Houts, R., & Morrison, F. (2007). Opportunities to learn in America's elementary classrooms. *Science, 315*(5820), 1795–1796.

Putnam, R. (2000). *Bowling alone: The collapse and revival of American community.* New York: Simon and Schuster.

Ramirez, G., & Beilock, S. L. (2011). Writing about testing worries boosts exam performance in the classroom. *Science, 331*(6014), 211–213.

Ratey, J. (2008). *Spark.* New York: Little, Brown.

Rattan, A., Good, C., & Dweck, C. S. (2012). "It's ok—not everyone can be good at math": Instructors with an entity theory comfort (and demotivate) students. *Journal of Experimental Social Psychology, 48*(3), 731–737.

Razza, R. A., Martin, A., & Brooks-Gunn, J. (2012). The implications of early attentional regulation for school success among low-income children. *Journal of Applied Developmental Psychology, 33*(6), 311–319.

Reed, J., & Ones, D. S. (2006). The effect of acute aerobic exercise on positive activated affect: A meta-analysis. *Psychology of Sport and Exercise, 7,* 477–514.

Reynolds, D., Nicolson, R., & Hambly, H. (2003). Evaluation of an exercise-based treatment for children with reading difficulties. *Dyslexia, 9,* 48–71.

Robb, K. A., Simon, A. E., & Wardle, J. (2009). Socioeconomic disparities in optimism and pessimism. *International Journal of Behavioral Medicine, 16*(4), 331–338.

Rogers, D. E., & Ginzberg, E. (1993). *Medical care and the health of the poor.* Boulder, CO: Westview Press.

Rothbart, M. K., & Bates, J. E. (2006). Temperament. In N. E. Eisenberg, W. E. Damon, & R. M. E. Lerner (Eds.), *Handbook of child psychology, Vol. 3: Social, emotional, and personality development* (6th ed.) (pp. 99–166). Hoboken, NJ: Wiley.

Rowe, G., Hirsh, J. B., & Anderson, A. K. (2006). Positive affect increases the breadth of attentional selection. *Proceedings of the National Academy of Sciences of the USA, 104*, 383–388.

Salminen, T., Strobach, T., & Schubert, T. (2012). On the impacts of working memory training on executive functioning. *Frontiers in Human Neuroscience, 6*, 166.

Sapolsky, R. (2005). Sick of poverty. *Scientific American, 293*(6), 92–99.

Sargent, D., Brown, M. J., Freeman, J. L., Bailey, A., Goodman, D., & Freeman, D. H. Jr. (1995). Childhood lead poisoning in Massachusetts communities: Its association with sociodemographic and housing characteristics. *American Journal of Public Health, 85*(4), 528–534.

Sauter, D. A., Eisner, F., Ekman, P., & Scott, S. K. (2010). Cross-cultural recognition of basic emotions through nonverbal emotional vocalizations. *Proceedings of the National Academy of Sciences of the USA, 107*(6), 2408–2412.

Schmader, T., & Johns, M. (2003). Converging evidence that stereotype threat reduces working memory capacity. *Journal of Personality and Social Psychology, 85*(3), 440–452.

Schultz, D., Izard, C. E., Ackerman, B. P., & Youngstrom, E. A. (2001). Emotion knowledge in economically disadvantaged children: Self-regulatory antecedents and relations to social maladjustment. *Development and Psychopathology, 13*, 53–67.

Senay, I., Albarracín, D., & Noguchi, K. (2010). Motivating goal-directed behavior through introspective self-talk: The role of the interrogative form of simple future tense. *Psychological Science, 21*(4), 499–504.

Sheridan, M. A., Sarsour, K., Jutte, D., D'Esposito, M., & Boyce, W. T. (2012). The impact of social disparity on prefrontal function in childhood. *PLoS ONE, 7*(4), e35744.

Shernoff, D., Csikszentmihalyi, M., Schneider, B., & Shernoff, E. S. (2003). Student engagement in high school classrooms from the perspective of flow theory. *School Psychology Quarterly, 18*(2), 158–176.

Silverman, M., Davids, A., & Andrews, J. M. (1963). Powers of attention and academic achievement. *Perceptual and Motor Skills, 17*, 243–249.

Skipper, J. I., Goldin-Meadow, S., Nusbaum, H. C., & Small, S. L. (2009, April 28). Gestures orchestrate brain networks for language understanding. *Current Biology, 19*(8), 661–667.

Slack, K. S., Holl, J. L., McDaniel, M., Yoo, J., & Bolger, K. (2004). Understanding the risks of child neglect: An exploration of poverty and parenting characteristics. *Child Maltreatment, 9*(4), 395–408.

Slepian, M. L., & Ambady, N. (2012). Fluid movement and creativity. *Journal of Experimental Psychology: General, 141*(4), 625–629.

Smith, J. R., Brooks-Gunn, J., & Klebanov, P. K. (1997). Consequences of living in poverty for young children's cognitive and verbal ability and early school achievement. In G. Duncan & J. Brooks-Gunn (Eds.), *Consequences of growing up poor* (pp. 132–189). New York: Russell Sage Foundation.

Söderqvist, S., Nutley, S. B., Peyrard-Janvid, M., Matsson, H., Humphreys, K., Kere, J., et al. (2012). Dopamine, working memory, and training induced plasticity: Implications for developmental research. *Developmental Psychology, 48*(3), 836–843.

Spiegel, C., & Halberda, J. (2011). Rapid fast-mapping abilities in 2-year-olds. *Journal of Experimental Child Psychology, 109*(1), 132–140.

Spilt, J. L., Hughes, J. N., Wu, J. Y., & Kwok, O. M. (2012). Dynamics of teacher-student relationships: Stability and change across elementary school and the influence on children's academic success. *Child Development, 83*(4), 1180–1195.

Stallard, M. L. (2007). *Fired up or burned out: How to reignite your team's passion, creativity, and productivity.* Nashville, TN: Nelson.

Steele, C. M., & Aronson, J. (1995). Stereotype threat and the intellectual test performance of African Americans. *Journal of Personality and Social Psychology, 69*(5), 797–811.

Steptoe, A., Wardle, J., & Marmot, M. (2005). Positive affect and health-related neuroendocrine, cardiovascular, and inflammatory processes. *Proceedings of the National Academy of Sciences of the USA, 102*(18), 6508–6512.

Taki, Y. (2010). Breakfast staple types affect brain gray matter volume and cognitive function in healthy children. *PLoS ONE, 5*(12), e15213.

Tasset, I., Quero, I., García-Mayórgaz, Á. D., del Río, M. C., Túnez, I., & Montilla, P. (2012). Changes caused by haloperidol are blocked by music in Wistar rat. *Journal of Physiology and Biochemistry, 68*(2), 175–179.

Taubert, M., Lohmann, G., Margulies, D. S., Villringer, A., & Ragert, P. (2011). Long-term effects of motor training on resting-state networks and underlying brain structure. *Neuroimage, 57*(4), 1492–1498.

Temple, E., Deutsch, G. K., Poldrack, R. A., Miller, S. L., Tallal, P., Merzenich, M. M., et al. (2003). Neural deficits in children with dyslexia ameliorated by behavioral remediation: Evidence from functional MRI. *Proceedings of the National Academy of Sciences of the USA, 100*(5), 2860–2865.

Thibodeau, L. M., Friel-Patti, S., & Britt, L. (2001). Psychoacoustic performance in children completing Fast ForWord training. *American Journal of Speech-Language Pathology, 10*(3), 248–257.

Thorell, L. B., Lindqvist, S., Bergman Nutley, S., Bohlin, G., & Klingberg, T. (2009). Training and transfer effects of executive functions in preschool children. *Developmental Science, 12*, 106–113.

Tomarken, A. J., Dichter, G. S., Garber, J., & Simien, C. (2004). Resting frontal brain activity: Linkages to maternal depression and socio-economic status among adolescents. *Biological Psychology, 67*(1–2), 77–102.

Trappe, H. J. (2010). The effects of music on the cardiovascular system and cardiovascular health. *Heart, 96*(23), 1868–1871.

Treadway, M. T., Buckholtz, J. W., Cowan, R. L., Woodward, N. D., Li, R., Ansari, M. S., et al. (2012). Dopaminergic mechanisms of individual differences in human effort-based decision-making. *Journal of Neuroscience, 32*(18), 6170–6176.

Trentacosta, C. J., & Izard, C. E. (2007). Kindergarten children's emotion competence as a predictor of their academic competence in first grade. *Emotion, 7*(1), 77–88.

Valentine, J., & Collins, J. (2011, April 11). *Student engagement and achievement on high-stakes tests: A HLM analysis across 68 middle schools.* Paper for the Annual Conference of the American Educational Research Association, New Orleans, Louisiana.

van Wouwe, N. C., Band, G. P., & Ridderinkhof, K. R. (2011). Positive affect modulates flexibility and evaluative control. *Journal of Cognitive Neuroscience, 23*(3), 524–539.

Vandrick, S. (2000, March 14–18). *Language, culture, class, gender, and class participation.* Paper presented at the Annual Meeting of Teachers of English to Speakers of Other Languages, Vancouver, British Columbia, Canada.

Wadsworth, M. E., Raviv, T., Compas, B. E., & Connor-Smith, J. K. (2005). Parent and adolescent responses to poverty-related stress: Tests of mediated and moderated coping models. *Journal of Child and Family Studies, 14*(2), 283–298.

Walker, D., Greenwood, C., Hart, B., & Carta, J. (1994). Prediction of school outcomes based on early language production and socioeconomic factors. *Child Development, 65,* 606–621.

Wang, C., Szabo, J. S., & Dykman, R. A. (2004). Effects of a carbohydrate supplement upon resting brain activity. *Integrative Physiological and Behavioral Science, 39*(2), 126–138.

Wang, Y., & Zhang, Q. (2006). Are American children and adolescents of low socioeconomic status at increased risk of obesity? Changes in the association between overweight and family income between 1971 and 2002. *American Journal of Clinical Nutrition, 84,* 707–716.

Wanless, S. B., McClelland, M. M., Acock, A. C., Ponitz, C. C., Son, S. H., Lan, X., et al. (2011). Measuring behavioral regulation in four societies. *Psychological Assessment, 23*(2), 364–378.

Weinreb, L., Wehler, C., Perloff, J., Scott, R., Hosmer, D., Sagor, L., & Gundersen, C. (2002). Hunger: Its impact on children's health and mental health. *Pediatrics, 110*(4), e41.

Wentzel, K. R., Barry, C. M., & Caldwell, K. A. (2004). Friendships in middle school: Influences on motivation and school adjustment. *Journal of Educational Psychology, 96*(2), 195–203.

Wild, B., Erb, M., & Bartels, M. (2001). Are emotions contagious? Evoked emotions while viewing emotionally expressive faces: Quality, quantity, time course and gender differences. *Psychiatry Research, 102*(2), 109–124.

Williamson, M. (1996). *A return to love: Reflections on the principles of* A Course in Miracles. New York: Harper Paperbacks.

Wu, M. (2012). *The irreplaceables: Understanding the real retention crisis in America's urban schools.* Available: http://tntp.org/irreplaceables/dcps

Xue, Y., Leventhal, T., Brooks-Gunn. J., & Earls, F. J. (2005). Neighborhood residence and mental health problems of 5- to 11-year-olds. *Archives of General Psychiatry, 62*(5), 554–563.

Yazzie-Mintz, E. (2007). *Voices of students on engagement: A report on the 2006 High School Survey of Student Engagement.* Bloomington, IN: Center for Evaluation and Education Policy, Indiana University. Available: http://ceep.indiana.edu/hssse/images/HSSSE%20Overview%20Report%20-%202006.pdf

Index

The letter *f* following a page number denotes a figure.

About the Author

Eric Jensen is a former teacher who has taught at all levels, from elementary school through university, and is deeply committed to making a positive, significant, and lasting difference in the way we learn. His academic background includes a B.A. in English and an M.A. in organizational development, and he is currently completing his Ph.D. in human development. He has authored 30 books, including *Teaching with the Brain in Mind, Teaching with Poverty in Mind, Turnaround Tools for the Teenage Brain, Enriching the Brain, Student Success Secrets,* and *Super Teaching.*

In 1981, Jensen cofounded SuperCamp, the United States' largest and most innovative academic enrichment program, now with more than 60,000 graduates. As a leader in the mind/brain movement, Jensen makes regular visits to neuroscience labs and is a member of the invitation-only Society for Neuroscience. Currently, he conducts staff development and summer in-depth trainings and speaks at conferences nationwide. For information on speaking dates or in-depth trainings, contact diane@jlcbrain.com or go to www.jensenlearning.com. And visit the website for this book: www.tools forengagement.com.

Related ASCD Resources: Engaging Students from Poverty

At the time of publication, the following ASCD resources were available (ASCD stock numbers appear in parentheses). For up-to-date information about ASCD resources, go to www.ascd.org. You can search the complete archives of *Educational Leadership* at http://www.ascd.org/el.

Professional Interest Communities
Visit the ASCD website and scroll to the bottom to click on "professional interest communities." Within these communities, find information about professional educators who have formed groups around topics like "Brain-Compatible Learning" and "Professional Learning Communities."

ASCD EDge Groups
Exchange ideas and connect with other educators interested in various topics, including Brain-Compatible Learning, Engagement and School Completion, and Inspiring Student Motivation on the social networking site ASCD EDge™.

PD Online
Achievement Gaps: The Path to Equity by Kathy Checkley (#PD09OC64)
The Brain: Memory and Learning Strategies, 2nd Ed. (#PD11OC112)
Embracing Diversity: Effective Teaching, 2nd Ed. (#PD11OC123)
Teaching with Poverty in Mind (#PD11OC139)
Understanding Student Motivation (#PD11OC106)
These and other online courses are available at www.ascd.org/pdonline

Print Products
Classroom Strategies for Helping At-Risk Students by David R. Snow (#105106)
Create Success! Unlocking the Potential of Urban Students by Kadhir Rajagopal (#111022)
Everyday Engagement: Making Students and Parents Your Partners in Learning by Katy Ridnouer (#109009)
How to Motivate Reluctant Learners by Robyn R. Jackson (#110076)
Inspiring the Best in Students by Jonathan Erwin (#110006)
Managing Diverse Classrooms: How to Build on Students' Cultural Strengths by Elise Trumbull and Carrie S. Rothstein-Fisch (#107014)
Meeting Students Where They Live: Motivation in Urban Schools by Richard Curwin (#109110)
The Motivated Student: Unlocking the Enthusiasm for Learning by Bob Sullo (#109028)
Teaching with Poverty in Mind: What Being Poor Does to Kids' Brains and What Schools Can Do About It by Eric P. Jensen (#109074)
Teaching with the Brain in Mind, 2nd Ed., by Eric P. Jensen (#104013)
Totally Positive Teaching: A Five-Stage Approach to Energizing Students and Teachers by Joseph Ciaccio (#104016)
Turning High-Poverty Schools into High-Performing Schools by William H. Parrett and Kathleen Budge (#109003)

DVDs
Motivating Black Males to Achieve in School and in Life by Baruti Kafele (#611087)
Teaching with Poverty in Mind DVD Series: Elementary and Secondary (#610135)

The Whole Child Initiative
The Whole Child Initiative helps schools and communities create learning environments that allow students to be healthy, safe, engaged, supported, and challenged. To learn more about other books and resources that relate to the whole child, visit www.wholechildeducation.org.

For more information: send e-mail to member@ascd.org; call 1-800-933-2723 or 703-578-9600, press 2; send a fax to 703-575-5400; or write to Information Services, ASCD, 1703 N. Beauregard St., Alexandria, VA 22311-1714 USA.